EFFECTIVE CORPORATE STRATEGY IN MANUFACTURING

George W. Plossl

George Plossl Educational Services, Inc., Marietta, GA 30067

Library of Congress Cataloging in Publication Data

Plossl, George W.

Production and Inventory Control.
Bibliography: p

1. Corporate strategy
2. Inventory control
3. Production control

1. Title: EFFECTIVE CORPORATE STRATEGY IN MANUFACTURING

LC Catalog No. 86-90412
ISBN No. 0-926219-03-0

Printed in the United States of America

DEDICATION

To Marion, Keith and Marian who each had a significant part in this family project. It may be as the old saw says that families that pray together stay together but we are absolutely certain that families that work together successfully are more tightly knit in all ways.

PREFACE

Top-level executives, middle managers, consultants and professors are all conscious of the problems of strategic planning; most of them are very verbal and many of them are diligent in publishing their thoughts about the strategies by which industrial firms should be guided. Strategies in the marketplace, in product design and in product line offerings are clearly necessary. Their influence on the health and growth of the company are direct and immediate as well as long-term. Today, financial strategies are having enormous influence on the way companies are being managed; the market value of its stock, its ability to attract or repel potential takeovers and cash flow are often more important to management than its performance in the marketplace.

In all of this strategic thinking, strangely, the strategies by which line manufacturing operations — the process of making the products — should be run have been largely ignored. Failures by plants to support marketing and sales strategies have been blamed on inept production managers. These have been the culprits also in high costs and excessive delays in introducing new products and processes. Manufacturing strategies too often are the result of the measures by which performance is judged — high efficiency of labor and high utilization of equipment, for example — which can easily be opposed to market strategy. Manufacturing strategy set by default like this will rarely be right.

The mission of manufacturing plants to support market and product line strategies can be carried out successfully only if they are operated to compatible strategies. The failure of many United States companies in international competition is the price being paid for managements' lack of understanding of this need. This book is intended to aid executives in manufacturing companies to develop better understanding of how their operations can and must be run to compete successfully worldwide.

Manufacturing is seen by most top-level managers as a welter of petty daily decisions requiring technicians with specialized skills working under extreme pressures. A decade of attempts to develop computer-based planning and control systems to improve their performance has changed managements' views from a hope of a "bright future" to a reality of many expensive and tragic failures. These have been blamed on the technicians to whom management delegated the systems development work without proper direction. The true responsibility lies with top managers, however, who avoided involvement in operational matters, who did not ask the right questions at crucial times and who failed to give proper direction to achieve the necessary coordination of the major groups in their organizations. These failures were the result of lack of understanding of how to run manufacturing plants rather than deliberate intent. It is my hope that this book will prevent some future failures.

Veritable libraries have been written on the subjects of planning and control and whole subdivisions of such libraries could be filled with the literature on the application of planning and control to manufacturing activities. Unfortunately, the bulk of these writings have been either so general as to be of only academic interest or so specific that they fail to reveal the broad picture needed by management to understand how to put these two activities to use effectively. This book presents an integrated overview of the subject in management language. At the same time, it includes enough technical detail to demonstrate how successful firms are putting the concepts to work.

The contents of this book have been drawn from the many years of experience that I have had personally, coupled with those of my associates in consulting and in conducting both executive and technical seminars on these subjects. It is broad enough in coverage to present the full spectrum of planning for operations in all industries. Yet it also contains enough detail so that those interested in understanding specific applications will find the material they seek. This book was not written to be read from cover to cover; it is intended rather as a reference work. The table of contents is quite definitive on the subject matter included. The bibliography contains references to the best sources of additional information on specific topics.

This book will provide materials useful in the major educational programs facing the management of industrial enterprises. Nothing contained in it is pure theory; everything has been tested in the crucible of manufacturing plants. An old adage says, "Everything comes to him who waits" but it may not be just what he wants. In the case of manufacturing, waiting may be fatal. If you would rather not wait, applying the concepts and techniques in this book will help you. Good luck.

GEORGE W. PLOSSL

TABLE OF CONTENTS

1. PERSPECTIVE, 1

2. THE PLANNING HIERARCHY, 4

3. STRATEGIC PLANNING, 8

4. BUSINESS PLANNING, 12

5. PRODUCTION PLANNING, 13

6. THE MASTER PRODUCTION SCHEDULE, 18
  - Historical 18
  - Definition 19
  - Objectives, 21
  - Relation Of MPS To Production Plan, 21
  - Sources Of MPS Data, 22
    1. Forecast, 22
    2. Unshipped Customer Orders, 22
    3. Changing Inventory Totals, 24
    4. Released Finished Goods Orders, 25
    5. Safety Stocks, 25
    6. Lot Sizing, 25
    7. Lead Times, 25
    8. Time-phased Order Points, 27
    9. Replacement Parts, 29
    10. Affiliate Plants Requirements, 30
    11. Process Limitations, 30
    12. Capacity Limitations, 30
  - The Horizon (time span) and the Time Period (bucket), 31
  - Master Production Schedule Zones, 33
  - The MPS Format, 34

7. MASTER PRODUCTION SCHEDULE VARIATIONS, 37
Major Products Built for Stock, 37
Many Products Built for Stock, 37
Major Units Custom-Built, 39
Many Products Made to Order, 39
Combinations of Stocked and Make-to-Order Products, 40
Products Sold As Is And Also Used in Higher Level Assemblies, 41
Continuous or High Volume Production, 43
Branch Warehouses, 43

8. INSURING THAT THE MPS IS REALISTIC, 45
Rough-Cut Capacity Requirements Planning, 45
Spare Parts Capacity Requirements Planning, 49
Affiliate Plant Capacity Requirements Planning, 49
Comparing Required and Available Capacity, 50

9. PLANNING VERSUS EXECUTION, 52
Relation of MPS to Other Plans, 52
Separating Planning From Execution, 54

10. THE PRODUCTION/DELIVERY RATIO, 62

11. MAINTENANCE OF THE MPS, 63

12. USES OF THE MPS, 65
Resource Planning, 65
Material Planning, 65
Capacity Planning, 65
Making Customer Delivery Promises, 67

Budgeting, 67
Profit Planning, 68
Monitoring Factory Performance, 69
Scheduling Engineering, 69
Coordinating Major Departments, 70

13. PROBLEMS WITH THE MPS, 73
Invalid Input Data, 73
Finishing Schedule Versus MPS, 73
Overstated MPS, 74
Nervousness of the Plan, 75
Level MPS Versus Level Work Center Loads, 76
Let The Computer Do It, 76

14. ORGANIZATION, 77
Top Management, 77
Design Engineering, 78
Marketing, 78
Finance, 79
The Master Schedulers' Job, 79

15. THE FUTURE, 81
A Changing Environment, 81
Just-In-Time, 82
Keys To Success, 84
1. Top Management Commitment, 84
2. Education And Training, 84
3. A Dedication To Continual Improvement, 84
The Requisite Redirection, 84

LIST OF ILLUSTRATIONS

1. MASTER PLANNING HIERARCHY, 5

2. PRODUCTION PLAN, 14

3. MPS DEVELOPMENT, 23

4. FIRM ORDERS VERSUS MPS, 24

5. TIME-PHASED ORDER POINT, 27

6. TIME-OFFSET BILL OF MATERIALS, 32

7. MASTER PRODUCTION SCHEDULE ZONES, 33

8. THE MASTER PRODUCTION SCHEDULE FORMAT, 35

9. CONVENTIONAL VERSUS INVERTED BoM, 42

10. BILL OF LABOR — Family #1, 46

11. ROUGH-CUT CAPACITY PLAN IN STANDARD HOURS, 47

12. SUMMARY ROUGH-CUT CAPACITY PLAN, 48

13. PLANNING VERSUS EXECUTION, 53

14. OVERPLANNING OPTIONS — MAKE-TO-STOCK, 57

15. OVERPLANNING OPTIONS — MAKE-TO-ORDER, 58

16. PRODUCTION VERSUS DELIVERY CYCLES, 62

17. MPS AND MRP, 66

18. COMPARING ACTUAL PRODUCTION WITH MPS, 69

19. LEVEL SCHEDULE #1, 83

20. LEVEL SCHEDULE #2, 83

EFFECTIVE CORPORATE STRATEGY IN MANUFACTURING

1. Perspective

During and immediately after World War II practically every major manufacturing company in the United States was directed by managers who felt they understood the manufacturing process. Our role as "the arsenal of democracy" was well earned in the prodigious output of airplanes, ships, guns and other wartime materiel. The morale and work ethics of American workers was very high; labor unions were not antagonistic and had relatively little power; and government was sympathetic and cooperative in assisting manufacturing in meeting the needs of the country and its allies.

When the war-starved consumer demand for automobiles, household appliances and other peacetime products was satisfied in the early 1950's the needs of industry changed from manufacturing expertise to a need for an understanding of markets and their creation and enlargement. Managers with these skills became the driving forces in industry.

The 1960's were characterized by great growth and prosperity. United States workers led the industrial world in productivity and American products dominated world markets. Labor unions grew in strength and influence and demanded a larger share of the pie. Government agencies no longer viewed industry as one of the major sources of real wealth but rather as polluters of the environment and threats to the health of workers and other citizens. Corporate taxes became a major source of money for redistribution to those more in need. Direct labor wages rose rapidly as did fringe benefits of all workers. The costs of safety devices and indirect taxes for welfare and medical plans escalated; industry, however, was able to pass the bulk of these cost increases along to their customers in higher prices so they felt no real pain.

In the 1970's other significant changes appeared. Managers with financial acumen saw benefits in mergers and acquisitions and the craze to develop conglomerates became the guiding rule of top level managers. Such managers has little understanding of manufacturing and how it should be operated and viewed such companies only as stocks and bonds in a portfolio to be manipulated for the maximum financial return to the conglomerate. Manufacturing managers who knew how operations should be conducted were now second-class citizens in the management hierarchy.

During these decades of the '50s, '60s and '70s the development of the computer and an understanding of manufacturing planning and control systems were also progressing rapidly. The basic principles by which manufacturing should be operated were identified, the necessary techniques for planning and control systems were developed and computer-based systems were installed in every progressive company. A few outstanding companies demonstrated the validity of the principles and the effectiveness of the techniques but these unfortunately were rare exceptions. The bulk of the money and efforts spent on such installations did not generate a small fraction of the potential returns.

The greatest single reason for these failures was the perception of these systems as the tools of the technicians in manufacturing rather than top management controls necessary to operate the total business. In addition, whole industries such as automotive, defense, aerospace and machine tools saw little application to their operations of the successful approaches in the more batch oriented types of production. They saw themselves as "different" and hence in need of entirely different control approaches. While these attitudes have been breaking down rapidly in automotive and process industries, they still prevail and prevent real progress in defense and aerospace companies and the machine tool industry is still suffering badly for its lack of attention.

The 1980s found much of U. S. industry in very serious trouble. Instead of learning how to develop operations into worldwide competitors, financially-oriented managers sold off assets to keep corporations financially healthy. Antagonistic take-overs and other financial manipulations diverted into the pockets of lawyers and bankers millions in capital which should have been appropriated for improving real wealth generation and capability in manufacturing.

The list of industries lost to international competition is well known and is still growing rapidly. The high-tech electronics businesses are proving to be no substitute for the heavy metal, smokestack type industries of the '60s and '70s. They are themselves falling victim to international competition. The service industries which so many seem to think provide the future earnings capabilities of the United States are still providing jobs for a growing labor force; since these do not generate real wealth, however, it should be obvious that they cannot be depended upon in the long term to support a rising standard of living for the growing population of the United States.

It is literally incredible that a nation with all the necessary ingredients for success in an industrial effort should be falling upon such hard times. The United States has the natural resources, the energy, the skilled and intelligent labor force, the transportation infrastructure and the large markets which are the basic requirements for a successful industrial effort. **The major lack is obviously one of qualified top-level management.**

We can no longer blame our troubles on high wages for direct labor. It is obvious in many industries that the elimination of all direct labor costs would still leave many United States firms non-competitive. The power and influence of labor unions are declining rapidly and, when faced with the reality of failures of companies, unions are cooperative in adjusting their demands and assisting management in the development of more competitive operations.

Government has yet to realize that real prosperity is impossible without a sound industrial base. It now provides little direct assistance to manufacturing. This does not require protective tariffs and restrictive import legislation; it involves rather a recognition of the prime importance of individual savings and capital investment to manufacturing activities, together with a reduced burden of uneconomic social programs which literally aggravate the situations they are designed to cure. Here top-level managers have defaulted on their responsibility to present strongly and clearly the necessities of sound manufacturing to the legislative and administrative branches of government.

The future will be fertile or futile depending on the ability of top-level managers in the United States to redirect their efforts in operating manufacturing companies. Instead of selling off operations at distress sale prices, redirection is needed to restore the financial health of such plants by operating them as they should be and can be run by competent, professional manufacturing managers. Manufacturing businesses are not loosely knit confederations of marketing, engineering, finance and manufacturing activities but are rather a single entity needing a unified, integrated effort with all of these functions working closely together toward common strategies. The United States must develop more chief executive officers, presidents and vice presidents who understand the "nuts and bolts" of manufacturing and can direct their teams of managers to develop worldwide competitive abilities.

2. The Planning Hierarchy

It is widely recognized and accepted that industrial companies need a variety of types of plans. Most management groups spend significant amounts of time in preparing these plans particularly in advance of the annual budgeting process. Thought is given to markets, to products and to facilities to produce them. Policies are established for customer service and stable employment among other corporate goals. The introduction of new technologies in both products and processes is considered.

Each major function — engineering, marketing, manufacturing and finance — considers matters carefully in its own areas of responsibility and expertise and these different considerations are merged into an integrated plan expressed in financial terms. The result, typically called "The Long Range Plan", is produced in a voluminous report and distributed to all managers who have a need to know and act on it. Unfortunately, most copies are carefully filed, not to be viewed again until just prior to next year's planning process.

Most companies lack true integration of the long range plan into operations. When this is so, the individual functions, while supposedly adhering to the long range plan goals and policies, in actuality are responding to day-to-day pressures and crises. This is not too strong an indictment of the planning process in many manufacturing concerns.

In the long range planning process, basic agreement is usually developed on such objectives as profits, rate of growth, customer service, share of market and return on investment. Serious differences among managers of the different functions arise, however, in the day-to-day actions necessary to reach these commonly agreed objectives. Marketing people see clearly that achieving desired levels of customer service and growth as well as share of market and profit depend upon having a wide variety of low cost products with new models introduced frequently and quickly, supported by inventories of necessary spare parts and adequate amounts of finished products always in stock.

Research and development and design engineering prefer to operate at their own deliberate paces to develop state of the art products with only minimal attention to marketability and produceability. To meet profit and return on investment goals in which they play the major role, manufacturing people wish for accurate forecasts, strive for stable plans, press for high selling prices and deplore the number and variety of new product introductions and engineering changes. It would appear that these groups were not operating to common strategies. This is more typical than not.

Long range planning in this spasmodic, disjointed fashion cannot be effective. The major functions of the company cannot be allowed to operate independently with the inevitable conflict of interests interfering with the effective execution of whatever plans are made. Excellence in operations requires an integrated, orderly hierarchy of master plans such as is

FIGURE 1
MASTER PLANNING HIERARCHY

PLAN/HORIZON	ATTEMPTS TO ANSWER
Strategic plan 5 - 10 years	What business are we in now? What markets do we serve now? What business do we want to be in? What other markets should we serve? What must be done now to get ready? By Engineering? By Marketing? By Manufacturing? What will be required next? Do all functions' strategies match?
Business plan 2 — 5 years	How do our products, markets rank now? Which are declining? How fast? Dropped? Which are mature, stable? Which are growing? How fast? What new products are needed? When? What are competitors doing? Products? Technologies? Applications? What actions are needed? When?
Production plan 2 — 5 years	How well is present plant utilized? Bottlenecks? Excess capacity? What demands will be made on it? What new technologies will be involved? When? What new products will be introduced? When? What products will be dropped? When? What new plant, equipment will be needed? When?
Master production schedule 1/4 — 1 year	What specific products are to be made? How many? When? What other materials are to be made? How many? When? What capacity constraints exist? Our facilities? Suppliers? What other constraints exist? Tooling? Space? Support staff?

illustrated in Figure 1. This shows four basic levels of plans — the Strategic, Business and Production Plans and the Master Production Schedule.

The figure shows also the typical questions which each phase of planning attempts to answer. The fundamental nature of the questions and the difficulty of getting quantitative answers are quite obvious. Also obvious is the universal applicability of the process to any type of business.

The strategic phase focuses on overall direction of the business, usually called its "charter". It is intended also to identify the major markets the company serves and the strategies to be followed by the functions of the business; an important objective is to insure that these strategies are compatible. It covers a horizon of a minimum of 5 years; the maximum rarely exceeds 10.

The business plan covers a much shorter horizon, usually no more than 5 years and often only 2. It concentrates on product families and their life cycles. It must be consistent with the front end of the strategic plan.

The production plan is developed simultaneously with the business plan and has the same horizon and time periods. Its primary objective is to insure that the necessary resources of capital, plant and machinery, people and materials are made available in time to support the strategic and business plans.

The master production schedule is the most detailed of all the plans and has the shortest horizon, rarely longer than one year. It deals with specifics of bills of material of existing and proposed products and recognizes constraints in executing plans. It drives all of the detailed day-to-day operating plans. The name is poor since it connotes order schedule dates and implies that it is part of the execution process. IT IS NOT. This will be covered in more detail later in this book.

Sound business and production planning are the primary requirements for effective control of any business engaged in manufacturing and distributing products. These plans are numerical statements of how the business will be conducted. Each is made in five phases, covering the individual activities of Research and Development, Design Engineering, Marketing, Manufacturing and Finance. Research and Development focuses on new technologies of products or processes. Design Engineering develops new products and major improvements in existing ones as well as assisting Manufacturing in the application of new process technologies. Marketing defines the company's role in the market place, methods of achieving desired share of market, channels of distribution, needed customer service levels and market needs and growth anticipated. Manufacturing provides the resources of plant and equipment, materials and people to support the market's needs and Finance provides the capital and controls to monitor how well the business is being managed.

The first year's data in these plans provide information to those concerned with hiring and developing people, procuring materials, buying short-lead-time equipment, making the products, planning inventory levels and detailed budgeting. Data for the second and subsequent years is used by those responsible for getting critical raw materials, long-delivery equipment and additional plant space, developing new markets and products, expanding the distribution network and introducing new technologies. The need for careful integration of these business and production plans cannot be overemphasized. Management time spent in this activity will have major impact on the health and success of the business.

3. Strategic Planning

Many managers accept the futility of attempting to make projections for their businesses more than a year in the future and do only a cursory, superficial job of attempting to identify future events which can affect their businesses significantly. Sound strategic planning does not attempt to identify a single set of data describing the future five to ten years hence. Rather it attempts to identify the various courses of action which might occur so that contingency plans can be made in advance to prevent crisis reaction at the last moment. No attempt should be made to specify what will happen in the future but rather to project the future effects of current decisions and to identify alternative plans to handle changes in direction as they become evident.

One of the most important factors in strategic planning is to develop a clear statement of the charter of the business, the type of business the company is in. Too often management identifies this with the products now being made — "we are in the forklift truck business" or" we make electronic home appliances". This is usually much too narrow a view and results in failure of the business to take advantage of new product and new market opportunities. It is interesting to speculate how the railroads in the United States would have developed had they seen their business not as simply "running a railroad" but as "providing transportation of people and materials". Instead of the products made, the statement of a company's charter should focus on the services rendered and the type of customers served.

In the strategic planning activities, careful coordination is needed of the work of the various functions. Research and development efforts must, of course, precede application design. Coordination of marketing and design engineering is vital if products are to have real market impact and to serve the real needs of customers. Engineering designs must be completed in time for procurement of necessary tooling, materials and other manufacturing facilities and manufacturing must be in action before sales can expect customers' orders to be filled.

For too long, management has been too tolerant of the inability of research and development and design engineering people to adhere to schedules. The United States space program, many military projects and breakthrough computer developments have all proven that schedules can be adhered to even for products not yet invented. Time is the one resource available to everyone but impossible to store. Losing time is the greatest waste we can experience. Around-the-clock operations for design engineering involving relatively few people are far less costly and much more productive than attempting to get back on schedule when many individuals and activities are involved in the procurement of materials and the manufacture of components and products.

Probably the most important factor in strategic planning is the insurance that the strategies of the various major functions are compatible. Marketing strategies are usually considered quite carefully in deciding how to respond to competition and opportunities in the marketplace. It is not unusual for companies to see the need for more varieties of products developed more quickly, short and on-time deliveries to serve a particular niche in the marketplace and fast response to changes in both product designs and customer requirements. It is equally common to find manufacturing measured on their ability to keep costs under control and to develop high utilization of expensive equipment and minimum waste of direct and indirect labor. In performing to meet such measures, of course, manufacturing will strive for stable operations and wish for good forecasts. They will resist the development of new models or products and the introduction of many engineering changes at frequent intervals.

It takes only a moment's consideration to see that the strategies of marketing and manufacturing in this example are directly in conflict. Add to this the desire of marketing for low costs to provide ample margins to help compete in the marketplace and manufacturing's interest in high selling prices to take the pressure off factory costs and competition instead of cooperation between marketing and manufacturing becomes very destructive.

Probably the single most important activity in strategic planning is the development of a clear statement of strategy for each of the major functions and the insurance that these strategies are compatible. This includes engineering, marketing, manufacturing and finance, the latter particularly because of the high interest in mergers, acquisitions and financial manipulations of whole corporations now so prevalent.

Typical of strategies developed for design engineering are:

1. Develop state-of-the-art technologies in both products and processes. This is typified by military and defense production and the so-called "hi-tech" products in electronics.
2. Insure top performance of product functions. This is characteristic of low-volume, high cost, high quality automobiles and commercial aircraft.
3. Introduce counter-cyclical products. These offset seasonal or other cyclical products and provide more balanced use of manufacturing facilities.
4. Aim for high facilities utilization. Some products are developed to replace others that have become obsolete or are introduced to give higher utilization of new and high technology facilities installed to take advantage of such capabilities.

Since the bulk of the material and production costs, the inventory investment and many manufacturing problems are determined by the product design, in-depth consideration of the manufacturability of products is essential in the design phase.

Marketing strategies can be one or more of the following:

1. Have low price/high volume products as is typical of household appliances, personal toiletries and many other consumer products.
2. Have products with top quality/top price/limited volume which is characteristic of high priced automobiles and porcelain art objects.

3. Have products in a broad line/many varieties/quick delivery. This is the type of strategy adopted by Stanley Tools and similar manufacturers to meet all of a customer's needs for their types of products. This helps keep competition out of the picture.

4. Have a narrow line/few varieties/fast response to customer changes. This strategy is adopted by companies attempting to enter markets dominated by major competitors such as IBM and General Electric. Head-to-head competition with such giants is avoided and only a portion of the market is served.

Inherent in the development of marketing strategies is the knowledge of the true needs of customers. These are frequently quite different from the needs perceived by engineering and marketing people and even from the wants expressed by customers. Close and open relations with customers is essential to define their real needs correctly.

Manufacturing strategies can include:

1. Produce high volume/low cost/limited varieties of products. This is most often seen in consumer products in so- called mass production.

2. Make products in wide variety/low volume/flexible response to market changes. This is typical of heavy machinery, off-road equipment and machine tools.

3. Make items of top quality/high performance/limited volumes. This is characteristic of such products as top-of-the-line automobiles, cameras, watches and stereo sound equipment.

4. Custom-built. This is the true job shop environment making products to individual customer specifications and usually in quantities of one or two.

Attempting to combine in one factory two or more strategies can be self-defeating. This has been seen clearly when companies previously concentrating on defense and military products have attempted to diversify into consumer goods. It is practically impossible to perform to two different strategies in the same manufacturing facility. This requires setting up separate and distinct facilities even though they may be under the same plant roof. Plants focused on a limited line of products with a single strategy guiding them will outperform the large industrial- complex facility every time.

Strategies in finance include:

1. Increase value per share of stock. This can require careful study of leasing vs. owning capital equipment, using funds generated internally rather than entering equity markets and selling off fixed assets.

2. Increase return on capital employed. Tight budgeting of expenses, programs to reduce inventories and accounts receivable and similar actions support this strategy.

3. Reduce Debt/Equity ratio. This focuses on reducing long- and short-term debt using funds generated internally.

The era of financial manipulations of manufacturing companies has not yet ended, unfortunately. Based on a fallacy — that plant operations cannot be made competitive — divestitures of companies that could have been salvaged have cost millions of dollars that could have been spent in rehabilitation. Enormous legal and banking fees in acquisitions and mergers for dubious financial reasons have siphoned off more millions of scarce and expensive capital needed for improvement of manufacturing operations. This has been a significant factor in the loss of competitive position by American corporations.

Some combinations of strategies among marketing, manufacturing, engineering and finance are obviously very compatible and others highly competitive. They need not be mutually exclusive; some strategies can apply to one line of products or one market served and others to an entirely different market or line of products.

Strategic planning should be an annual effort occupying the attention of the top level management group. It also needs to be reviewed for possible changes quarterly or no less than twice a year. The output of this planning effort should be:

1. A specific statement of strategy for each of the major operating functions — marketing, engineering, manufacturing and finance — for the various major families of products and markets.
2. Attempts to answer each of the questions in Figure 1 for strategic planning. These answers may be specific or just a generalized statement depending on the nature of the question.
3. Identification of alternative courses of action and some generalized contingency plans to handle each alternative.
4. Specific time tables for the major activities in the first year or two (depending on the type of business) of the planning horizon to be coordinated closely with the business and production planning activities to be described next.

4. Business Planning

Business planning has a shorter horizon than strategic planning and focuses on product families and share of market. Like strategic planning, business planning is not intended to develop specific numbers in a time frame. Its purposes are to indicate trends, to set minimum and maximum dates for introduction or ending of the production of specific products and to develop timetables and details of marketing and sales activities to improve the company's competitive position.

While a separate phase of planning, the business plan cannot be developed independently of the strategic plans already made; they must be tied closely together and support each other. As in strategic plans, the first one or two years at the front end of the business plan are shown in more detail and with more specific data so that the subsequent detailed planning processes can be integrated better with them.

As noted in Figure 1, a specific question of business planning is the actions of competitors in introducing new products, discontinuing old ones, and developing new technologies or new applications in the marketplace. Here more specific answers are sought. The actual performance and, even more important, the intentions of competitors are vital questions in determining a company's plans for its products and markets.

Such intelligence can be gained in a variety of ways. Mutual customers can reveal competitors' actions or intentions consciously or inadvertently. Trade association meetings and publications are sources of such information. Capital investments in new facilities in new areas or in plant expansions are often revealed by equipment suppliers, banks or real estate brokers, tipping off competitors' product or market strategies. Mutual suppliers can divulge competitors' inquiries or orders for new and different materials and direct industrial espionage is not unknown.

The business plan, for each of the major product families, attempts to identify where each product is in its life-cycle — growing, mature, or declining. An important decision which seems to be extremely difficult to make is when to declare a product obsolete. Particularly when the present management has been responsible for its introduction, there is often extreme reluctance to drop a product from the line. This contrasts dramatically with the first action usually taken by a parent company which acquires another — review each product line to see what items should be dropped from production.

The steps in business planning are:

1. Develop accurate data on actual product sales.
2. Analyze products for life-cycle position.
3. Determine competitors' actions and intentions.
4. Prepare specific plans for improving viable products.
5. Prepare specific plans for phasing out obsolete items.

5. Production Planning

The strategic plan focuses on markets and long range trends, the business plan looks in more detail at the company's and competitors' products and the production plan views manufacturing facilities to support both the strategic and business plans. It's horizon is the same as that of the business plan and, like it, is much shorter than that of strategic plans.

The production plan is greatly influenced by product life-cycle considerations developed in the business plan and must be integrated tightly with it. It must also be integrated closely with the strategic plan since the necessity for fast response in the marketplace and flexibility in introducing and manufacturing new products places specific requirements on plant capacity and equipment.

Since it deals with the facilities needed, an important consideration in production planning is the identification of components and products which will be purchased from outside sources or manufactured internally. Also important is the determination of which components and products will be made in which facilities in the multiplant environment.

Production planning data are frequently utilized foı the physical capital budget development. The quantities and time frames used and the questions answered will, of course, be much more specific than those in business and strategic planning.

The objectives of production planning are:

1. To determine the resources needed to support the business plans. These include plant, machinery, equipment, materials, people, capital and the services of outside suppliers.
2. To set time tables for the actions of marketing, design engineering and research and development needed to support the business and production plans.
3. To provide summarized data for top management to measure the performance of all the functions in executing the business and production plans.
4. To insure that the resources are applied properly to attain the desired levels of customer service, inventory, profit and other objectives of the total business.

A typical production plan is shown in Figure 2. This is a composite of production plans for each of the 14 families of products, the repair parts and the interplant transfer components. This plan really shows the interaction of sales, production and inventories. Sometimes called an S-P-I Report the bottom of Figure 2 shows clearly that inventories at the start of a period plus production during the period minus period shipments at cost will equal the inventories at the end of the period.

This is typical of make-to-stock operations where inventories provide a buffer between production and shipments. In a make-to-order environment the customer order bookings backlog provides a similar buffer so that production does not necessarily equal shipments in any given period.

It is a rare business where production can be turned on and off to match customer demand. The larger and more complex the operations, the more it is necessary to attempt to achieve some stability in the total production output.

One of the most difficult tasks in running a manufacturing facility is to achieve a smooth, balanced flow of materials through the various operations in sequence. Changing production levels inevitably destroys this balance and incurs significant costs as well as other penalties when the balance is destroyed.

FIGURE 2
PRODUCTION PLAN

Month	Jan.	Feb.	Mar.	Oct.	Nov.	Dec.
Family #1 (Units)	5500	5600	5600	5200	5300	5300
Family #2 (Units)	500	550	350	300	400	450
" " "						
" " "						
" " "						
Family #13 (Units)	100	100	—	—	—	—
Family #14 (Units)	—	—	100	110	120	130
Repair Parts ($000)	250	250	250	280	280	280
Interplant Trans. ($000)	160	160	160	160	160	160
Begin'g Invent. ($000)	1153	1110	1083	991	1058	1104
Production ($000)	1038	1074	1037	1015	1048	1037
Cost of Sales ($000)	1081	1101	1121	951	981	991
Net Sales Value ($000)	2162	2202	2242	1902	1962	1982

The production plan shown in Figure 2 is made for a variety of product families. These should be the broadest possible product groups which go through similar manufacturing operations. Choosing such groups correctly requires a thorough knowledge of the plant's manufacturing processes.

The product groupings selected for production planning are rarely the same as those significant to marketing or to the inventory control group. The groups must be meaningful in terms of their demand on the manufacturing facilities. The production plan shows the rate at which such product families will be manufactured but it is not intended to be a commitment to individual items within each family.

Figure 2 shows units and dollars as the unit of measure for the quantities of each product family in each time period. The units of measure selected should be those most meaningful to the people operating the facilities who need to make and manage the changes. Typical of measures commonly used are:

1. Units — pieces, tons, gallons, dozens, doses and others which express quantities of products.
2. Equivalent units — making allowances for the varying sizes and complexity of products within a family. For example a dual service station pump capable of putting fuel into two vehicles simultaneously would be equivalent to two single pumping units.
3. Financial terms — dollars or other currencies which may be the only other possible compromise for families of great varieties such as repair parts and sets of material transferred between plants.

The specific steps required in making a production plan are:

1. Determine the families to be grouped together.
2. Determine the horizon and the time periods to be included in the plan. Many companies make a total plan such as Figure 2 showing overall monthly figures for the first year and quarterly data for the second. Data for additional years are usually in half-year or total annual requirements. For individual product families, supporting plans are then made in weekly increments for only the first year.
3. Set a minimum inventory level for products made to stock and a minimum customer order backlog for make-to-order items.
4. Determine the sales forecast totals for each product family over the planning horizon. Since family totals are used these will be more accurate figures than sales forecasts for specific models or items within each family.
5. Determine the total inventory available at the beginning of the planning period for families of products made- to-stock and determine the total customer order backlogs at the beginning of the planning period for those families made-to-order.
6. Set the desired inventory level and customer order backlog level at the end of the period for the corresponding products. Considerations in determining these levels are discussed in References 19 and 20 in the Bibliography.
7. Calculate the total production required for the planning period. This will be the sales demand total plus or minus the difference between the beginning and ending inventories.
8. Spread the total production over the full horizon as desired. This will involve consideration of months with a significant number of holidays, plant vacation shutdowns, interruptions in production for plant expansions or moves and seasonal products.

Product family #2 in Figure 2 indicates seasonal requirements. The production rates have been changed several times during the year. This may or may not be the best way to handle seasonal products. When making such a production plan three alternatives are available:

1. Hold a level production rate which will require rather high levels of inventory to be built during the off-peak selling season; these will supply the needs of the peak demand.
2. Minimize inventories by changing the production rate frequently to meet the seasonal sales demand.
3. Some combination of these two extremes with fewer changes made in production rate to minimize both excess costs and excess inventories.

Basically a seasonal production plan attempts to balance the investment in excess inventories against the additional costs of changing the production level. Unfortunately few of these costs can be estimated precisely and some less tangible factors may be equally important. For a detailed discussion of such factors see "Production and Inventory Control: Principles and Techniques", Second Edition, Reference 19 in the Bibliography.

There are significant advantages to being able to offset one seasonal family with another having the opposite cycle so that total demand on the facilities is fairly uniform during the year. Unfortunately it is not easy to do and is not common in industry. Seasonal production plans really are an attempt to store labor at the lowest total cost.

Higher level skills such as machining, welding, blending and other operations (usually producing components) are both more expensive and less flexible. Finishing operations including subassemblies, assemblies and packaging tend to be lower cost and more flexible. It is good practice to maintain fairly level schedules of the skilled labor activities producing excess inventories of components which are then used at varying rates to finish into products as required to meet the sales demand.

Some additional considerations in making production plans are:

1. Plans should be made for each manufacturing facility and suboperation which is or could become a bottleneck.
2. Picking the right measures of capacity to use is important since they should provide the most meaningful possible information to those individuals charged with changing production rates and managing the operations.
3. It is frequently useful to show cumulative sales and production figures instead of detailed figures for each time period. Cumulative data permit comparisons of actual sales and production to the planned figures as time goes on. It would be a mistake to insist that a plant meet a planned increase in production rates if sales in total were not up to the forecast and the inventory was therefore higher than planned. On the other hand, production at the planned rates would be inadequate if sales were exceeding the forecast totals causing inventories to drop below planned levels. Looking at the three factors — sales, production and inventory — together in a production plan in aggregate is the best method for establishing sound control of manufacturing operations.

4. Some finite period of time is required for changing production levels and the information on necessary changes must be given to those responsible for making them soon enough to plan for the necessary actions.

5. Production plans should be changed only when necessary. Some sets of rules should be established ahead of time indicating when production level changes will be made. Such rules would include inventory being above or below targets by some specified percentage, sales exceeding forecast levels by some specified amount or production being below or above planned levels by more than a specified tolerance.

Production planning is not a precise process nor does it use specific detailed information which many managers prefer. For this reason it tends to be neglected. This is unfortunate because a sound production plan used to establish good control over flow rates of product families can be the most important of all planning information.

The production plan is the basic device for integrating fully the marketing, engineering, manufacturing and financial plans. It provides aggregate information in summarized form making it easier for management to review the performance of the various functions against their individual plans. It should be a vital element in the management process.

6. The Master Production Schedule

Historical

Master Scheduling is not a new activity or concept. It was used extensively in the earliest material control systems in conjunction with the "quarterly ordering system". This system took a backlog of customer orders and converted it to a production plan for the next 3 months (hence the name). The production plan was then "exploded" manually to determine parts requirements and these parts purchased or manufactured at the proper time. It has long been in use in many companies making machine tools, aircraft, ships, locomotives and heavy machinery, where customer order bookings provide long period backlogs or where the delivery schedule is reasonably firm as in defense contracts and military procurement.

The quarterly ordering system, and with it the master production schedule, dropped out of use in most companies, however, as product variety proliferated, order backlogs decreased and procurement lead times lengthened. When backlogs shrank below the minimum needed to cover the time for procurement of necessary materials and production of the end product, the plan had to be based partly on forecasts. These, of course, were rarely accurate and actual demand differed significantly from plan. Resulting changes to the manufacturing plan had to be re-exploded to determine revised parts needs but this took too long when done manually. Before one change had been processed, the next one had arrived. The system was just too slow and cumbersome to survive.

About this time in the mid-1950's a great interest developed among academicians and consultants in the application of the techniques of probability and statistics to inventory management. Statistical forecasting techniques like exponential smoothing were developed and combined with the statistical analysis of forecast error for the calculation of safety stocks. This reasoning led to the development of order points (also called reorder points, order review points and min-max) based on two factors. The first was the expected demand during the projected lead time for replenishment of the item. The second was a buffer stock or safety stock based upon the potential variation in this expected demand over the replenishment period.

Statistical analysis of past history of each item was used to calculate its own safety stock to give a level of assurance of a given amount of customer service, usually expressed as a percentage. A basic assumption was made that this would provide better control than calculations based upon bills of material and schedules for the finished products. Since such calculations could not be made and updated often enough in practice, the order point approach was adopted by most companies attempting to improve the management of inventories.

Although it improved results over the use of rules of thumb and other guesstimating techniques, the order point technique failed in its objective when applied to items related in bills of material as components of a product. At its best it succeeded in keeping some of almost everything around all the time. As it planned parts one by one, with no concern for how these parts were linked in bills of material, it caused unbalanced inventories with simultaneous excesses and shortages. It had another major failing: once an order was released, it was impossible to develop revised "need dates" as schedules changed and other upsets occurred.

Also in the late 1950s, the business computer became available for use in inventory management. This tool made it possible to use the technique now called Material Requirements Planning (MRP), really the same in concept as the quarterly ordering system. The right technique had been reborn because of the capabilities of computers to handle the masses of data required to explode a master production schedule, determine parts requirements quickly and, even more important, process changes and replan economically.

Material Requirements Planning requires an input of a set of numbers defining what is to be produced, how many and when; it then explodes these numbers into parts requirements by time period. However, the real value of MRP is much more than providing a material ordering technique; it also maintains valid need dates on all orders outstanding, as well as providing input data (planned orders in the future) to capacity planning.

Using a sales forecast to provide the input to MRP works reasonably well as long as the total of the demand forecast is within the capabilities of the plant to produce. As soon as forecast demand exceeds capacity, however, using the forecast to drive MRP triggers more orders than the plant can handle, generating excessive numbers of "Past Due" orders which completely destroys the ability of MRP to keep priorities of open orders valid.

It is evident that there has to be an interface between the sales forecast and MRP which considers capacity limitations of the plant as well as other factors that can cause a difference between what is forecast to be sold and what is able to be produced. This role is performed by the Master Production Schedule (MPS).

Unfortunately in too many companies, master schedule development was seen as a clerical task necessary only to provide some input to run MRP programs. It was not seen in its true light as a part of the overall master planning process. The role of the master production schedule in linking the production plan to the day-to-day operations was overlooked. Also ignored was the need for top level managers to be familiar with master scheduling and the use of the data in detailed planning. This combination of neglects is probably the single largest reason why modern planning and control techniques on powerful computers have failed to generate their true potential benefits.

Definition

The term Master Production Schedule has had different meanings for different people.

General agreement has developed among practitioners on a definition which has appeared frequently in MRP literature and is included in the Certification program of the American Production and Inventory Control Society. This is the definition that will be used here:

> A master schedule is a set of numbers determining what will be made, how many will be made and when they will be made. It is a manufacturing plan, not a sales plan. It must consider the total demands on a plant's resources, including finished product sales, spare (repair) part needs and interplant (affiliate company) needs. It must also consider the capacity of the plant and its vendors to meet these needs. It provides the overall plan for each manufacturing facility's operation. All detailed planning for materials, people, plant, equipment and other resources required for manufacturing the products will be driven from the master schedule.

A key point to consider in this definition is that it is not a "schedule" in the literal sense. Each entry in the MPS consists of a quantity of an item identified by a bill of materials and a time bucket. Entries are often made in the MPS to plan for sets of lower level parts but no firm commitment is made to produce the parent item. Rather than being a schedule, it should be thought of as a set of planning numbers.

It should also be understood clearly that the MPS is not a part of the execution process. An MPS should be viewed as a plan to work from, not a schedule to work to. If significant changes become necessary as time passes, the MPS provides a base set of numbers from which to determine quantitatively and specifically what materials and work centers are affected.

The MPS is, therefore:

1. A planning device, part of the planning hierarchy.
2. A statement of what should and can be made. It is, therefore, a matrix of items scheduled showing the time periods covered for each item so scheduled. The time periods used most often are weekly although occasionally bi-weekly or monthly periods are used for large, complex products like power generation equipment, ships and aircraft. Those people more knowledgeable in the power of computers than in the needs of master production schedules advocate daily time buckets; these are completely impractical and, while they may be more precise, they cannot be more accurate.
3. A way to balance customers' needs against plant capabilities. The MPS cannot be a wish list of what a company's management might like to produce. The problems resulting from overstating the MPS are both immediate and serious and are discussed in detail later in this book.
4. A means for management control of the workforce, plant, equipment, materials, finances, engineering and marketing programs.
5. A way to coordinate all functions of the business.
6. A basis for measuring the performance of each function.

The MPS is not:

1. A collection of sales forecasts.
2. A summary of customer orders for products.
3. Assembly schedules for detailed production.
4. Packaging schedules.
5. Part of the execution process.

Objectives

The objectives of Master Production Scheduling are:

1. To provide top management with a means to authorize and control manpower levels, inventory investment and cash flow, giving them a real handle on customer service and profitability.

2. To provide a mechanism to coordinate marketing, manufacturing, engineering and finance activities so they all work together to achieve a common performance objective.

3. To provide a device to reconcile the needs of marketing with the capabilities of manufacturing.

4. To provide an overall measure of how well each major function in the business is able to make a sound plan and then execute it.

5. To provide input data to programs developing detailed material, capacity and financial requirements.

6. To provide a means to make more reliable delivery promises to customers and to evaluate the specific effects of changes in delivery schedule

Relation of MPS to Production Plan

The MPS and the Production Plan represent two significantly different levels of detail needed in planning a company's manufacturing operations. The production plan is expressed in more general terms and units of measure summarized by groups or families of products. It has a longer horizon than the MPS. A primary use of the production plan is in determining limitations in resources which would prevent meeting the output goals so that these limitations can be overcome in time. In the near term the production plan serves as a summary for management of detailed plans which must, of course, fit more closely with available resources.

The Production Plan also reflects top management's policies in inventory management, customer service and the stability of production as well as in growth rates. It also integrates the more detailed plans of the major functions of the business and as such represents an agreed consensus among the top level managers of these functions on conflicting policies and strategies.

The Master Production Schedule, on the other hand, is more detailed, applies to specific products or sets of components described by bills of material and deals with a shorter time frame in more precise time periods. It reacts to changing product mix and other short range considerations that are not reflected in the production plan but must still be constrained by the overall rates set by the production plan. The MPS initiates many specific actions such as buying materials, scheduling the procurement of machinery and equipment and hiring people. Top management must be actively involved in its development and use, in seeing that it integrates well with the production plan and that the details support all policies, strategies and objectives.

Sources of MPS Data

Some very specific data are needed to create the MPS. These data may be of greater or lesser importance, depending on the type of industry and the company's processing sequences and stocking plan. Here are the major elements that should be considered in developing any master schedule:

1. Forecast — For companies building or buying finished products, components or raw materials to be held in stock in advance of receipt of customer orders, the MPS needs as part of its input a forecast of future demand. This forecast must cover, or be convertible into, the same items, time periods and units of measure as the MPS (such as specific products, families, options or accessories) and provide quantities by time period associated with each. The forecast must also extend over a horizon far enough into the future to meet the needs of the MPS and MRP. The level of detail for the products defined in the MPS may change as the horizon extends farther and farther into the future as discussed in the following section — "The Horizon and Time Period," Page 31. The forecast should lend itself to making this transition. There is no alternative to making a forecast of future demand unless the backlog of firm customer orders extends beyond the required minimum MPS horizon. Someone has to estimate the demand on which to base the manufacturing plan if customers will not wait the full cycle of procurement and processing of the required materials.

2. Unshipped Customer Orders — In a very few businesses, the horizon of unshipped customer orders is far in excess of the time period required to procure the necessary raw materials and components and produce the finished products. This is typical of defense, aerospace, heavy machinery and some companies which dominate their markets. In such businesses no forecasts are necessary; the firm customer orders make up the Master Production Schedule. In every make-to-order business and often in make-to-stock companies, there is a backlog of customer orders not yet shipped. Contrary to most popular literature and discussions about blending orders and forecasts, these orders should NOT be substituted for the master production schedule quantities. A comparison of actual orders and forecasts should be used to determine whether or not the master production schedule needs to be revised. Otherwise firm customer orders should be treated as part of the execution process, not the planning process.

Figure 3 shows how firm orders can be compared to forecasts and a current master schedule reviewed for possible revision. Prior to Week 15, actual sales of product #4321 must have been slightly below forecast. This is shown by the Available figure in Week 15 being 120 instead of the 100 which would have occurred had actual sales and forecast totals been equal. The firm order line for Weeks 15, 16 and 17, however, shows that actual sales during this period have been well above the forecasted total of 50 each week. As a result, projecting forward from the current Week 18, it is apparent that the Available will drop below zero in Week 20 and be well below the projected safety stock level of 100 units. Also the Available To Promise quantities in Weeks 20 and 23 will be well below the forecasted total of 50 units each week. This suggests a potential revision to the Master Production Schedule. One alternative would be advancing the 150 quantity from week 21 to 20 and scheduling each subsequent MPS quantity one week earlier. Before this revision was actually made, however, the master scheduler and material planner would check the feasibility of producing the quantities one week earlier than planned.

FIGURE 3
MPS DEVELOPMENT

Product #4321 **On Hand = 120** (Now) **Safety Stock = 100**

Week	15	16	17	18	19	20	21	22	23	24
Forecast	50	50	50	50	50	50	50	50	50	50
Available	120	62	0	95	45	-5	95	45	-5	95
Current MPS	150	—	—	150	—	—	150	—	—	150
Firm Orders	58	62	55	—	—	—	—	—	—	—
Avail. to Prom.	162	100	45	145	95	45	145	95	45	145
Revised MPS	—	—	—	150	—	150	—	—	150	—

The example in Figure 3 is for a product made-to-stock with some planned safety stock. Finished goods inventory, including a quantity of safety stock, will usually cover unexpectedly large demand in one period and be replaced when demand in a succeeding period is below forecast. The MPS then functions as a finished goods replenishment system and can be buffered effectively from variations in customer order input. Changes in the forecast, actual sales different from forecast and planned changes in finished goods inventory levels would be considered in master scheduling this kind of item.

For make-to-order products, a comparison of booked orders against the master schedule could be viewed as "consuming" the master production schedule. In other words, specific customer orders are allocated against quantities in each time frame of the MPS and the unsold balance is viewed as a forecast of additional orders to be received during this period.

Note that this unsold balance provides the quantity "Available to Promise" on new customer orders. A simplified example of this is shown in Figure 4. If the MPS contains 50 units in Period 5 and there are customer orders in-house for only 35 units in this period, an added quantity of 15 is being "forecast" for this period. The basic assumption is that the forecast and MPS will match each other and additional orders will be received to make up any deficits unless a management decision is made to change the MPS.

FIGURE 4
FIRM ORDERS VERSUS MPS

Product #3322

Weeks	1	2	3	4	5	6	7	8	9	10	11
Master Schedule	—	50	—	—	50	—	—	60	—	—	60
Booked Orders	—	50	—	—	35	—	—	10	—	—	0
Unsold Balance	—	—	—	—	15	—	—	50	—	—	60

This approach requires that some customers wait for their products if they request delivery earlier than the time period in which they can be slotted. Using this method, the forecast must be tracked carefully to detect significant variances in rates of incoming business compared to the MPS, so that adjustments to the production rate can be planned as soon as necessary. As quantities in the MPS remain uncommitted to customer orders in near term periods, the question must be faced, "Will these be ordered yet? Later? Ever?"

Some companies use only firm customer orders through a given time period, say two months. After that, only forecast data are used, except in those specific periods where customer orders exceed the forecast, in which case the customer order total is used. This approach is not bad when the master schedule covers specific products that can be forecast. It is not good, however, when the product is custom made and the forecast is for a "typical product" or for a "planning module" (See the section on bills of material under "Problems With The MPS", Page 73). By ignoring some actual customer orders now in-house but scheduled in periods in which only forecast data are used, requirements for unique parts could be overlooked and such components poorly planned. Also the total plan, using the greater of forecast or customer demand, may exceed available capacity.

In comparing actual customer orders and forecasts and determining a potential revision to the master production schedule, joint discussions of questionable data in the MPS by manufacturing and marketing will provide the best results. This detailed analysis of specific situations by both groups will lead to better trade- offs and decisions than the application of arbitrary rules and standard logic.

3. Changing Inventory Totals — Finished goods inventory levels are changed for various reasons. A new warehouse or a new distributor may have been added and need

stocking. Finished goods inventories in some product lines may be deemed to be too high and need reducing or vice versa. These changes in inventory levels must be considered in developing the MPS. To reduce inventory, production must be less than sales; to increase inventory, production must exceed sales. The MPS drives production and must reflect desired changes in inventory levels of stocked finished products.

Even products made to order are affected by inventory decisions. Many times assemblies, components or materials are planned in excess of known demand to provide fast reaction to orders from important customers. Such inventory strategy will affect the MPS in the same way and be handled by the same logic as is used for make-to-stock items.

4. Released Finished Goods Orders — Replenishment orders for some of the end products in an MPS may already be released to manufacturing but not yet finished. Although these are part of the execution process, these orders will provide products to meet future sales and must, therefore, be recognized in the generation of the MPS. They are not part of the MPS which will be exploded to determine component requirements, however, since their parts will have already been allocated or issued. Released orders for each item must be known so that additional replenishment orders can be planned properly when evaluating or revising the MPS. These released orders are a firm commitment of the plant's resources, at least for the amount of work left to be done on the order, as well as a firm plan to make a quantity of product in a definite time period. The balance of work left on these replenishment orders must be considered when evaluating the capacity demands of the MPS.

5. Safety Stocks — In operating inventory replenishment systems, a quantity of finished goods inventory, designated as "safety stocks", may be planned to cover actual customer demand that exceeds the forecast. To preserve them for unplanned requirements, safety stocks are usually deducted from the actual on-hand quantity of finished goods to determine the quantity available to meet existing and new customer requirements and the timing of planned replenishment orders. These orders are then considered in developing the MPS. As with the finished goods inventory, it is changes in the safety stock levels which are of interest in developing the MPS. Production will have to be increased above customer demand to generate more safety stock and vice versa.

6. Lot Sizing — Money can be saved on changeover and setup of machines and work stations by making product in production lots or "economic order quantities". These lots may be calculated by formulas or picked for other reasons; for example, the batch of product that keeps a packaging machine busy one shift or the quantity of components which fill up an assembly station's containers. The MPS must be stated in these lot-sizes so that sets of components will be planned properly to be available to support assembly, finishing or packaging.

7. Lead Times — The time between the start of a replenishment order and delivery of finished materials into stock ready for use may involve assembly, testing, bottling, labeling,

packaging, or similar operations required to complete the product. The finishing lead time may also include the time to ship the product to branch warehouses. This lead time relates the date for issuing the replenishment order to the need date for the finished item. The MPS needs to know when it is necessary to issue replenishment orders to make products since this is the time the components will be needed and should be withdrawn from stock.

Two options are available when stating quantities of product in a master production schedule. The quantities may represent finished products, packaged and ready for shipment to customers or they may represent simply the quantities of matched sets of parts needed to begin the finishing process. If the former option is selected, the lead time for the finishing operations must be included in the top level of the bill of materials for the product so that the necessary offsets indicating the time to issue components and begin final assembly will be correct. If the second option is chosen and the MPS describes only sets of parts, then the finishing times must be added to the lead times expressed in the formal planning system when developing delivery promises for customers and planning capacity requirements for work centers involved in finishing operations.

The second option is often selected when finished products have many common components and the MPS can be stated in many fewer items. Manufacturing operations for semi-finished products or intermediates for chemicals or pharmaceuticals are most flexible when held in bulk in a few varieties and later finished into many unique items via simple machining, assembly, coloring or packaging operations. One of the basic objectives in making a realistic MPS is to level the workload on the high-skill areas of the plant, usually the earlier stages of product manufacture. The assembly order issue date and the finishing lead time determine the requirement date for components made in these earlier stages of manufacture. If these assembly start dates in the MPS cause an imbalance of work in the high-skill areas, they should be adjusted to give a more level load. This does not mean that assembly orders will actually be issued exactly as stated by the MPS; they represent the second phase of planning and control - execution. Adjusting the MPS in the first phase allows the lower level items to be planned better in early production operations. Assembly orders can be issued later to match the true sales demand and adjustments made in priorities of orders in secondary and subassembly operations to react to these changes.

8. Time-phased Order Points — A technique which can be helpful in preparing data for the MPS is the Time-phased Order Point. This is sometimes called by those who like buzz words, "Distribution Requirements Planning". It can be used in all make-to-stock situations and some make-to-order businesses also. An example of a time-phased order point for a stocked product is shown in Figure 5. Those familiar with material requirements planning will recognize that this uses the same general logic and format as an MRP printout. The only difference is that the requirements in the time-phased order point come from a forecast; in MRP they come directly from the MPS or are calculated from the planned orders for parent items at the next higher level in the bill of materials.

FIGURE 5
TIME-PHASED ORDER POINT

Forecast = 20/period **On Hand = 80**

LT = 2 OQ = 100 **SS = 55**

Period		1	2	3	4	5	6	7	8
Requirements		20	20	20	20	20	20	20	20
Scheduled Receipts		—	100	—	—	—	—	—	—
Available	25	5	85	65	45	25	5	-15	-35
Planned Order Due		—	—	—	—	—	—	100	—
Planned Order Release		—	—	—	—	100	—	—	—

Figure 5 develops a finished product replenishment plan from the data included in the header section. The "Requirements" line is a forecast of customer orders (sales). "Scheduled Receipts" shows the open replenishment order for this product, indicating both the quantity of the order and the period this amount is due into stock. The "Available" line begins with the on-hand quantity minus safety stock and then projects this quantity into the future, subtracting the forecast demand in each period. Open replenishment orders (Scheduled Receipts) are added to this Available figure in the period they are scheduled to be completed. This gives a picture of available inventory at the end of each period, if everything goes as planned.

"Planned Order Due" is calculated from the previous line. When all available inventory is consumed by the forecast requirements, a new order is needed and is planned for this period in the lot- size previously established. The next planned order is calculated to arrive in the period in which the last of the previous batch is consumed by the forecast and so on until the end of the planning horizon. The "Planned Order Release" is offset from the Planned Order Due by the lead time to make the product, indicating when work should be started in final operations.

The planned order release line is the suggested master production schedule for this item. This is a key point, the forecast of sales is NOT the MPS. It is important, for a number of reasons, to understand this difference clearly, the most significant being reduction of unnecessary "noise" in MRP and the need to consider capacity in the MPS. A forecast is an estimate of the average demand for an item over several periods in the future. The early users of MRP and, even today, many computer packages let forecasts developed by their programs set requirements for finished goods inventory, calculate planned orders and explode them through the bills of material. As these data change, MRP generates the normal exception reporting indicating that it is time for releasing, expediting and delaying open orders.

Figure 5 shows a forecast of 20/period with a planned order for 100 to be released in Period 5. One period after this plan was developed, conditions have changed from those planned. Suppose that 26 were actually sold in Period 1, taking one unit from safety stock. The Available inventory line will be reduced by 6 pieces, and will be negative in week 6, moving the Week 7 planned order of 100 automatically to the left one period for both the Due and Release lines. Exploding this change through MRP produces many exception messages, requesting expediting and early release of other open orders.

Suppose that Period 2 now passes and actual sales were 14 (indicating that the forecast average of 20 is a good figure). This immediately returns the Available inventory line to its original figures, the planned order for 100 shifts right one period and the MRP messages now suggest delaying the orders released and expedited last week. This "nervousness" could have been avoided easily by using the 55 safety stock. That is what it is there for but the system had no way to do it. Only by stabilizing the planned order releases in the time-phased order point can this be done. This is possible by using a "firm planned order" discussed in Reference 19 in the Bibliography or by manual intervention between the time-phased order point and the MPS. However it is done, the "noise" of forecast errors must be blanketed from MRP.

Further adjustments to the suggested MPS may be necessary when the schedules for all products are looked at in aggregate. Perhaps the suggested MPS overloads a section of the plant, develops very erratic loads in critical work centers or calls for materials vendors cannot deliver on time. To develop a realistic MPS, adjustments will have to be made to the planned order releases. If the Plant or vendor capacity is exceeded, the total quantity planned will have to be reduced to suit the capacity and material available. The schedule dates of planned orders will have to be shifted to solve the "peaks-and-valleys" problem. The later section, "Insuring That The MPS Is Realistic", Page 45 will cover this in more detail.

When using time-phased order points for make-to-order products, there are some significant differences. On-hand and safety stock quantities are usually zero since everything that is built gets shipped. The requirements line contains not only a forecast but also any unshipped customer order backlog. Another frequent, but not necessary change, is the elimination of lot quantities. As the product will be built to customer order, it is common to use the lot-for-lot technique, making in each period only enough product to fill the orders. Some make-to-order products are made periodically in batches, though, such as specialty chemicals processed in a batch because of kettle sizes, or special alloys and metal shapes produced and rolled in minimum quantities to spread over more units the setup cost of changing over furnaces and rolling mills. A lot-size may also be used to plan sets of lower level parts. A lot-size of 10 for a specific customer- selected option in the MPS will call for lower level items to be made in multiples of this quantity. Apart from these differences, both make-to-stock and make-to-order products are treated essentially the same and the time-phased order point works well for both.

9. Replacement Parts — Spare parts, repair parts, service parts and maintenance parts are different names given to parts necessary to repair finished products already in the hands of the customer. Bearings, seals, hoses, etc., are typical items in this group but it could also include large components such as replacement engines, transmissions, power packs, etc. The major problems with this group are the large number of parts that must be planned and the highly erratic demand experienced for many of them. They cannot be handled as a family because they are so diverse in processing and material content and cannot be reviewed individually because of their number.

The normal approach is to forecast spare parts individually but then treat them in two different manners. If they are no longer used in current production, a time-phased order point can be applied mechanically to handle each part. The planned order releases to replenish inventory would be the MPS input to MRP for planning procurement of subassemblies and manufactured parts. Essentially they are treated as "many products made to stock" discussed later under "MPS Variations", Page 37. They suffer from the same problems of forecast changes and actual sales differing from forecast as discussed. However, they rarely have enough importance to spend time reviewing each one individually. Many companies recognize this by isolating those repair parts that are assemblies or subassemblies and, therefore, could affect a large number of parts. These items only are elevated to master scheduled status and reviewed carefully to minimize nervousness. Master schedules for the other spare parts, purchased items or components, are allowed to fluctuate as actual sales differ from forecast and attempts are made to cope with the nervousness which results.

If they are still used in current production, the forecast of spare parts sales alone is the MPS for this independent portion of the item's demand. This forecast will be combined with the dependent requirements for such parts calculated by MRP from the explosion of the MPS for the finished goods. Hence, total requirements are developed to satisfy both assembly and replacement part needs. Again, important assemblies and subassemblies are manually controlled to minimize the noise level in MRP; other items are allowed to fluctuate as necessary.

For those spare parts sold only infrequently where average forecasts may be grossly inaccurate, two approaches are used: first, wait to receive the order before starting manufacture and quote delivery based on the full lead time required; or second, attempt to carry a minimum stock on hand which is replenished using the order point technique.

The tough problem with spare parts is in determining the total demands these parts will place on capacity and hence whether or not the overall plan is realistic. This is discussed more fully in the Section "Insuring That the MPS is Realistic", Page 49.

10. Affiliate Plants Requirements — Many companies have multi-plant operations where some of the production process occurs at one plant, the material is then sent to another for further processing and maybe to a third for finishing. This is very common in the textile industry and not unusual in chemicals and hard goods manufacture. Many companies have overseas operations or licensees that assemble products from components, some manufactured here and some procured locally. This demand on a plant's resources has to be considered in the MPS along with all others. For clarity, the terms "user plant" and "supplier plant" will be adopted to describe this relationship.

Two approaches can be followed. The first is to set up special (some say "partial") BoMs for each product listing only the parts furnished by the supplier plant. The user plant can then furnish its MPS to the supplier plant for these "products". It should be offset into earlier time periods to allow for transportation time and the user plant's lead time and then added to the supplier plant's MPS for its own products.

The second way is to centralize the planning for both plants. Develop the MPS to suit the demand of the market place as well as possible within the capabilities of both plants to produce. Include both supplier and user plant parts in one bill of material. The detail planning for materials in the supplier plant will come directly from the user's MRP explosion of a single MPS. We strongly recommend the second approach if the user plant takes a significant portion of the output of the supplier plant. When two plants are so interdependent, the supplier plant should be treated as a distant work center of the user plant. Other approaches will result in two MPS's that may not mesh well together making it difficult to achieve the overall goals of the company.

11. Process Limitations — Many processes control the way products will be scheduled. Dyes, inks or chemicals made in a variety of colors should be scheduled light, medium then dark through the tinting process to minimize the time required to clean out equipment. Furniture, manufactured traditionally with "cuttings", must be planned carefully to balance the work loads on turning, carving, veneer and finishing departments. These process limitations are an integral part of master schedulers' deliberations.

12. Capacity Limitations — Among the most important inputs needed to develop an MPS is information on capacity available to produce the necessary materials. Data are needed on finishing capabilities, which can vary widely with product mix changes and may often be easily increased or decreased if little skill is required in the operations. Information is also needed on output capabilities of the early stages of manufacture as well as on the volumes of materials obtainable from vendors. A detailed discussion of evaluating actual capacity is beyond the scope of this book; however, rough-cut methods of determining capacity needed to support the MPS are covered later in the section, "Insuring That The MPS Is Realistic", Page 45.

The Horizon (Time Span) and the Time Period (Bucket)

The horizon of a master production schedule is the length of time it extends into the future. The minimum required, as shown in Figure 6, is the cumulative lead time to procure material, make parts and assemble them into products. As shown, some raw material has to be bought, converted into specific fabricated components, processed further into sub-assemblies and then assembled into a finished product for sale. The longest such sequence establishes the minimum horizon for the MPS. The time offset bill of materials used in Figure 6 is a very easy way to determine this longest sequence for any particular product. Computer software programs have been developed to generate this information directly.

This time span is usually changing. When lead times expand, the horizon has to be extended and vice versa. A variable horizon in a company's MPS, however, is not practical. The past several years' experience in a business will show how the cumulative lead times have changed. A minimum horizon should be selected to handle the longest expected cumulative lead times. Common practice is fifty-two weeks although some companies have seventy-eight weeks or even more. If current lead times are short, the MPS horizon would not have to be filled completely.

There are some cases where the MPS data are deemed of very low reliability in the later periods of even its minimum horizon. If the minimum horizon is not filled with some data, requirements cannot be calculated via MRP to initiate release of orders for raw materials and other long lead time purchased items at the bottom of product bills of material. This is typified by the tubing #4785 in Figure 6. One alternative to using such data is to apply order points on these parts as an order launching mechanism to release orders based on estimated usage of the material. However, the actual need dates in the plant for these parts can be monitored and maintained valid by MRP as they move within the planning horizon. Thus, the true priority of the orders "launched" by the order point system can be given by MRP to the vendor or plant before the delivery date arrives.

FIGURE 6
TIME-OFFSET BILL OF MATERIALS

Pencil Assembly

```
WEEKS
 0   1   2   3   4   5   6   7   8   9  10  11  12  13  14  15  16  17  18  19  20  21
------------------------------------------------------------------------------------
 •       •           •           •           •   •               •       •

 * Assemble Pencil (#1200)
 •       * Get Rewind Mechanism (#2151) --- * Order Rewind Mechanism
 •       * Make Body (3440)  •           •   •               •       •
 •       •           •  * Get Tubing (#4785) ------------------ * Order Tubing
 •       * Make Cap Assembly (3151)      •   •                       •
 •                   * Get Lock (#2193) -- * Order Lock              •
 •                   * Get Insert (1102) -------- * Order Insert     •
 •                   * Get Button (#4430) ---- * Order Button        •
 •                   * Get Clip (#2587) --- * Order Clip             •
 •                   * Make Barrel (#5874)                           •
 •                               * Get Tubing (#4785) ------------------ * Order
 •                                                                         Tubing
 •
 •  ------------------------ MINIMUM MPS HORIZON ------------------------
```

Another way of solving the inadequate horizon problem is to forecast the demand, not for the lowest level parts in the BoM, but for sub-assemblies or higher level groupings, sometimes called modules or kits. This may be a better place to predict demand because of commonality of usage, and an MPS created here will ensure that matched sets of components are planned.

The final choice is to make the forecast at the finished product level even though the future is cloudy. The decision on which of these three alternatives to choose depends on where the best numbers can be generated. If the product is made from common raw materials and is mature and stable, forecasting at the bottom of the BoM might be best. However, if the product has a highly varying mix of materials and components and an unstable demand, then plans should be formulated at higher levels in the BoM.

The time bucket used in master schedules is usually one week. This determines the sensitivity of priorities in the MRP system. In very high speed or short lead time operations, it may be necessary to go to a daily time period or even to a single shift when many operations are completed within this period. For very long manufacturing cycles, such as in shipbuilding, this time bucket probably could be longer, maybe two weeks or even a month. Even if long time periods are used in the MPS and MRP, individual orders can be scheduled more precisely but this requires more complex programs. Large time buckets in the MPS also give less precise comparisons to determine capacity limitations.

Bucketless or dating systems remove these objections but the user should beware of the aura of precision they suggest. Remember that the master schedules in MRP are part of the planning process where precision is not necessary. When execution is involved, however, it becomes necessary to put more precise dates on orders and time periods into capacity decision making.

Master Production Schedule Zones

The Master Production Schedule, together with the Production Plan, is intended to provide information to those responsible for procuring the necessary resources. The basic lead times to obtain such resources vary considerably from very short to very long term. Figure 7 shows some of this schematically. Manufactured materials can be obtained in relatively short periods. Work force changes need rather significant time periods to implement and long lead time purchased materials and equipment take even longer. Plant buildings and machinery are usually the longest type of procurement items. It is possible to use different lengths of time buckets in these different zones.

For example, the first 26 weeks would provide fairly definitive information on the timing of procurement of the manufactured materials, work force and purchased materials. Over the balance of the one year total horizon the time periods could be months or even quarters since this information would probably be precise enough for planning procurement of long range machinery and plant buildings. During the short range, where more precise data are

FIGURE 7
MASTER PRODUCTION SCHEDULE ZONES

1 2 3 4{ }10 11 12 13{ }23 24 25 26{ }49 50 51 52

Manuf. Material

Workforce

Purchased Raw Material and Equipment

Long Lead Time Machinery & Plant

needed for priority planning, a weekly time bucket is most commonly used. In the intermediate zone where work force and capacity information together with raw material commitments are needed, however, a monthly time bucket is frequently employed. In the long-range zones, quarterly periods are probably most common.

However, material requirements planning has some problems with the variable-length time bucket, occurring at the transition between each range. For example, because of lead time off- setting in MRP, as the explosion proceeds down each level of the BoM, a quantity in a quarterly bucket in the long-range zone must be converted to monthly quantities in the intermediate zone and then to weekly quantities in the short-range. This conversion could be made using a 3-month per quarter or 4-week per month standard divisor but such averages may be unrealistic if lot- sizes are large. Most companies keep all data in weekly buckets and have the computer summarize it into monthly and quarterly totals in the proper zones for printed reports or displays. Of course, this limitation in "bucketed" systems does not exist in "bucketless" or date-controlled MRP systems.

Identifying the proper zones for a company and creating the MPS for these zones will simplify the planning job immensely. The approach that is almost universally taken of defining the master production schedule throughout its entire horizon in terms of the specific finished item or the finished accessory is of questionable value. If these times zones are recognized, significant benefits can be achieved by making better forecasts to feed the master production schedule and in creating and maintaining it.

The MPS Format

The MPS is simply a file where data can be stored for use in other programs. Many different formats are possible to use; the selection of a particular one will depend on the product line, the type of business, frequency of the revisions, how long the MPS has been in use and similar factors. The format of master production schedule files has been confused greatly in the literature with files of data used in the development of the MPS (such as Figure 3 in this book) and also with time-phased order point formats used in developing the MPS (shown in this book as Figure 5).

A spread sheet format similar to that shown in Figure 8 is a very useful layout, especially in companies just getting started with master scheduling as well as in those with a limited number of products. The sheet is a matrix with time periods horizontally and products listed vertically.

FIGURE 8
MASTER PRODUCTION SCHEDULE FORMAT

All Data In Units

Month		**February**					**November**		
Week	**5**	**6**	**7**	**8**	**( )**	**44**	**45**	**46**	**47**
Item A	50	—	50	—	( )	55	—	55	—
B	610	610	610	610	( )	610	610	610	610
C	340	360	380	400	( )	300	310	320	330
D	185	185	185	185	( )	140	140	140	140
E	15	—	—	—	( )	—	—	20	—
F	205	205	205	205	( )	225	225	225	225
G	—	—	5	—	( )	10	—	—	—
Family Total/Mo.		5600					5300		
Prod. Plan Total/Mo.		5600					5300		

The MPS quantities are placed in the proper time periods for each product. It is easy to see the data with this approach and to make trade-offs when needed. This enhances communications among sales, manufacturing and other departments. The data must be converted into computer readable form after each approval; this may become expensive and time-consuming if revisions are frequent and new products are added often. Its excellent readability and the ease of communication with top management, though, make it a most desirable format to use.

An MPS file for the multitude of products commonly found in manufacturing companies requires the use of a computer to maintain the data. Unfortunately, the ease of altering the computer files has given many the impression that master production schedules should be changed readily for all kinds of conditions. This ignores the significant difficulties that would be experienced in manufacturing plants and their suppliers in attempting to react to the changes easily made in the computer programs. This subject will be covered in more detail later in this book under the sections, "Separating Planning From Execution", Page 54 and "Problems With The MPS", Page 75.

Many companies attempt to maintain on the MPS file information on actual customer orders received as well as actual production output. This is a great mistake. Such actual data for comparison with the plan are better maintained in separate files such as Figure 3 for the development of an MPS, the time-phased order point file, Figure 5, or Figure 18 comparing actual with planned production. Changing basic data in MPS files is a serious activity and should be done only by a limited number of people and after careful consideration.

The MPS file format in Figure 8 shows units of products to be made in each of the weeks and a total for the family of similar products for the month. This monthly total is the figure to compare with the production plan shown in Figure 2 to insure that the detailed day-to-day operations plan is integrated closely to the longer range production and business plans. A good plan will have tolerances on the differences permissible between these two numbers. Variations outside the tolerance should be approved by top management before any revisions are made to the MPS.

7. Master Production Schedule Variations

The master production schedule is handled somewhat differently depending on the industry, the type of product and whether it is sold from stock or made to customer order. The handling of repair parts demands and interplant (affiliate) requirements was discussed in the earlier section, "Sources of MPS Data", Page 29 and 30.

1. Major Products Built for Stock — This includes some chemicals, textiles, major home appliances, farm equipment and construction machinery. The MPS for this group is usually made at the finished product level. Time-phased order points can be created for each of these finished products to generate the planned orders the plant must produce. The planned orders then become the suggested MPS for these products after being reviewed and adjusted as discussed under "Sources of MPS Data", Page 22 and in "Time Phased Order Points", Page 27.

A feature of many of these products is high seasonality, where significant percentages of the annual sales take place in a relatively short period. The plant, for economy and practical reasons must run on a relatively level basis. The seasonal forecast, when fed into the time-phased order point, will generate planned orders with a seasonal bias. These must be leveled out to match the plant's needs and ability and to determine the inventory swings needed to buffer the seasonal sales from the level plant output. For a further discussion on seasonality see the section, "Production Planning", Page 13.

2. Many Products Built for Stock — This includes toys, garments, textiles, pharmaceuticals, hand tools, small home appliances, rubber products, bearings, gears, chain and many other items. The major problem in master scheduling these products is the large number of different end products to handle; 5,000 to 10,000 catalog items are not uncommon. The amount of work necessary to create and maintain an MPS for each of these products dictates that a quick way be found to handle the data. Where possible, the best approach is to group like products into a family and develop an MPS for the family, with some mechanical way to determine each item's portion of this MPS. As an example, a hand tool manufacturer makes over 150 hammers, different in style, weight and handle type. It can also produce dozens of different screwdrivers, rules, planes and other tools. A separate MPS developed and reviewed manually for each style and size hammer, screwdriver, rule and plane is just not feasible. Hence, the MPS must be developed for families of products.

Hammers, over a range of weights, form one family in which the items require similar processing. The inventory of each hammer in the family is summed to get the total inventory for the family. A forecast is made for the family as a unit and the MPS is created for the family. The specific quantity of individual hammers to be produced is calculated based on historical percentages of sales of each hammer in relation to the family. Alternatively, a bill of materials for the family can be created, listing all the individual items in the family with the percent of sales as the "quantity per assembly". This allows the master schedule and its capacity effects to be analyzed manually and adjusted if necessary. The breakdown into specific orders for each item is then accomplished mechanically on a computer.

This approach, using the percentage of an item relative to a family total, works well where the items in a family are made from common raw materials. A good example is a set of gears cut from the same gear blank but having different bore configuration and number and style of teeth. Changes to the historical percentages affect only the gear to be machined next; they will not affect material procurement. However, if the percentage technique is applied to quite different items, different in both material and capacity needs, changes to the percentages will cause nervousness in MRP and possible inability to ship specific orders from stock. In such cases, the percentage changes should be implemented at a time selected in advance to give the plant time to adjust to the new data. Minor percentage changes should also be blocked from affecting MRP, again to minimize "noise".

Using a Pareto analysis will permit controlling the "significant few" differently from the "trivial many". In this approach, time-phased order points would be generated for all products but the "A" items would be reviewed manually and stabilized. The "B" and "C" items would not be reviewed; their planned orders would be adjusted automatically by the computer program. The concept used here is to control the bulk of the capacity demands, not the bulk of the part numbers, and let the actual demand for the latter come as it will. The danger here is that the "B" and "C" items, controlling the bulk of the part numbers, will interfere with the higher priority "A" items. This would be especially severe if the total demand for all items exceeded the available capacity.

Another way involves developing a system to give only exception reporting to get a manageable number of action notices. This technique generates a time-phased order point for each finished product and converts early period planned orders into "firm planned orders", essentially "freezing" the early horizon. The length of the frozen period would depend on the stacked lead time of the items as well as on how dynamic a company wants to be in the market place. (For additional discussion of freezing the MPS and using time fences, see the later section, "Separating Planning From Execution", Page 54). As actual demand differs from forecast, the safety stock is monitored. Logic rules such as, "Allow safety stock to be depleted 50% for 'A' items, 75% for 'B' and 100% for 'C' before flagging a part for review," are programmed. The reverse, warning of an over-stock condition, is also required. This effectively dampens much of the trivial noise and allows only significant changes to be flushed to the surface for manual review.

An alternative is to monitor the available inventory in periods on either side of the firm planned order due dates. If available inventory one period prior to the firm planned orders for "A" items goes negative, flag it, but flag "B" items only if 2 periods prior are negative and "C" items 3 periods. A similar set of rules is necessary to warn of over-stock potential. Which of these two techniques is selected is determined by the desired level of service to customers. If a company ships direct to customers and wants high service levels, safety stock monitoring is probably best. Those shipping to distributors or warehouses might prefer inventory monitoring.

3. Major Units Custom-Built to Order — Aircraft, ships, buses, truck trailers and specialized machine tools fit this grouping. The major characteristic of these products is the presence of a substantial customer order backlog. The variety of products these companies can make, each one custom-designed, precludes making heavy investment in materials or labor without knowing the specifics of the actual order. The customer order backlog then becomes the MPS. When the order backlog is large enough to cover the minimum MPS horizon, no additional demand data from forecasts may be needed to develop the MPS. When there are not enough orders to fill the MPS over the lead time required to procure materials and build the product, there are two alternatives. First, load the MPS with the actual customer orders booked and make plans to reduce the manning levels and procurement rates to match available orders. New orders will be quoted for delivery at the stacked lead time to make the item ordered. The staff will be built back up again as demand picks up.

The second alternative is to forecast customer demand and develop the MPS for basic elements that are repetitive in the product line. The basic elements may be as simple as lists of raw material normally used, could involve actual sub-assemblies of the product or could be "planning modules" that tie together components in the product related to customer options. These modules may or may not be built as a unit. An example of the latter would be air conditioning units for a truck where the planning module would include the compressor, cooling coils and vents but could also include such related items as tinted glass, heavy duty radiator, heavy duty battery and oversized fan and pulleys. (For more details on structuring bills of material in master production scheduling, see the later section "Problems with the MPS", Page 73.) Creating the MPS for this planning module based on forecasts of future demand would plan sets of component parts to be started through material procurement and manufacturing cycles in advance of receipt of customer orders. New customer orders could be quoted for delivery at the lead time necessary to complete the production of such modules and build them into the final product. The risk is that these modules will not be ordered by customers at the forecast rate and will have to be carried in inventory, reworked or become obsolete. These costs could be balanced against the costs of hiring or layoffs when making significant changes to the work force. Selecting which alternative to use would depend on the length of time the shortage of customer orders was expected to last, as well as competitors' performance. A much better solution, when the customer order backlog is not large enough to cover the minimum manufacturing cycle time, is to cut the manufacturing lead times. This is discussed later under the heading "The Future", Page 81.

4. Many Products Made to Order — Automobiles, hoists and machine tools are prime examples of this category. The biggest problem here is the combination of options that are possible and the resulting huge array of final products that can be made. The automobile, when its options are arranged in various combinations, can be built in billions of different finished cars. Obviously, the MPS cannot be stated in terms of the finished product.

The technique used is to develop an MPS for basic modules, like the body, accessories or options, as separate units based on forecasts for these modules. A forecast for a total number of full-size cars can be used as input to develop the MPS for basic modules. A forecast for the total number of each basic style of car can be subdivided to indicate the breakdown into 2-door sedans, 4-door sedans, station wagons and other models. These forecasts can be converted to an MPS for each body module which is exploded through the corresponding bills of material to determine component requirements. Similar procedures are followed for other modules such as engines, transmissions, rear ends, chassis, electrical systems, and brakes. The ideal is to be able to associate each customer option with a module.

A key to getting this approach to work is proper structuring of the BOM. This is the technique of grouping items related to each option into a separate BOM and developing an MPS for each and is discussed in more detail later in this book under "Problems with the MPS", Page 73. When this MPS is "exploded" through MRP, all the related parts will be planned as a set, not individually.

Using this approach requires different handling of a comparison of actual customer orders with the MPS from the ways already discussed. Customer orders specify all the options on the car and carry a unique number. The fully assembled car, though, will not appear on any MPS. To relate each order to the proper MPS for the various modules, the finished car order must be exploded to identify all options and accessories with modules. The MPS for each module would then be assigned its portion of the customer order. This same technique would be used when quoting delivery promises to customers. After receipt of the order, the specific modules would be identified and the latest available one would be the "gating" item for quoting the delivery date. (See "Making Customer Delivery Promises", Page 67).

There are many products made to order that do not fit the options or modular approach. Examples are windows, truck and off-highway vehicle axles and specialty chemicals. The percentage technique discussed earlier for use with many products built for stock is one that can assist here also, especially combined with over-planning. Customer orders are used for the short range portion of the MPS; families of products are used beyond this. The family is broken down into specific material and parts needs through the percentages calculated either on historical sales, current booked orders or combinations of these. Over-planning the family will provide additional material, allowing flexibility to react to specific demands in the short term. This is dangerous where unique parts having long lead times are buried in the family and care should be taken to plan these separately.

5. Combinations of Stocked and Make-to-Order Products — There are products which overlap the previous categories. Some products have a semi-finished level where stocking can occur but the finished items cannot be completed until the customer order is received. An example of this would be radio transmitters, where the frequency is not known until the customer order is in- house. The basic radio without frequency-related components

can be assembled as scheduled by its MPS as if it were a stocked product. The parts unique to the frequency, though, would be grouped in a module with a separate MPS and planned like a make- to-order product. Chemicals and paints that can be produced in bulk as intermediates but cannot be finished and packaged until receipt of the customer order are handled similarly. Products of this type are frequently known as "Assembled to Order" or "Finished to Order".

6. Products Sold As Is and Also Used in Higher Level Assemblies — Examples of these are fine chemicals, where an intermediate level is sold as a product and also used internally to make other finished goods. Another example is hand tools which are sold singly and are grouped into various combinations and sold as sets. Towels, sheets, pillow cases and many other consumer products follow this same pattern of individual sales plus sales in groups.

One way of developing the MPS for these products is to forecast individually the sales of the sets as well as the individual product sales and apply time-phased order points to the sets. During the MRP explosion, at the proper level in the BOM, add the forecast of independent demand for the products sold individually to their dependent requirements to make sets. Hence the total needs will be covered. This is similar to planning for repair parts also used in current production. Another approach is to forecast the total sales of each individual product, combining demand for those sold in sets and those sold individually, and create the MPS for the total sales of each item. The disadvantage of this approach is that packaging materials like cans and tool boxes cannot be planned since they will not appear in any BOM exploded from the MPS.

To get around this, portions of the BOM can be inverted as shown in Figure 9. This works well for products made in bulk and sold in a variety of package sizes such as aspirin, photographic film and many toiletries, pharmaceuticals and chemicals. The traditional

FIGURE 9
CONVENTIONAL VERSUS INVERTED BoM

Conventional Bill of Materials:

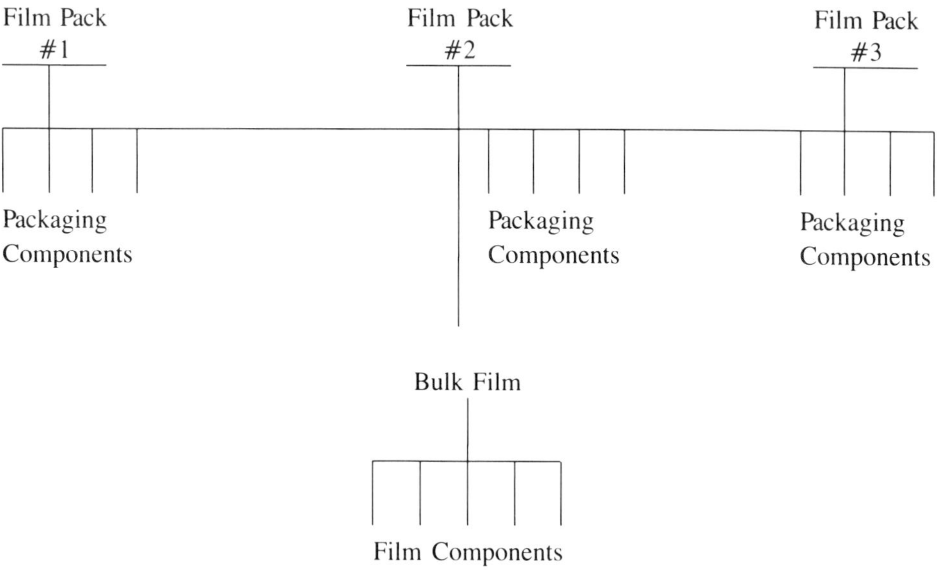

Inverted Bill of Materials:

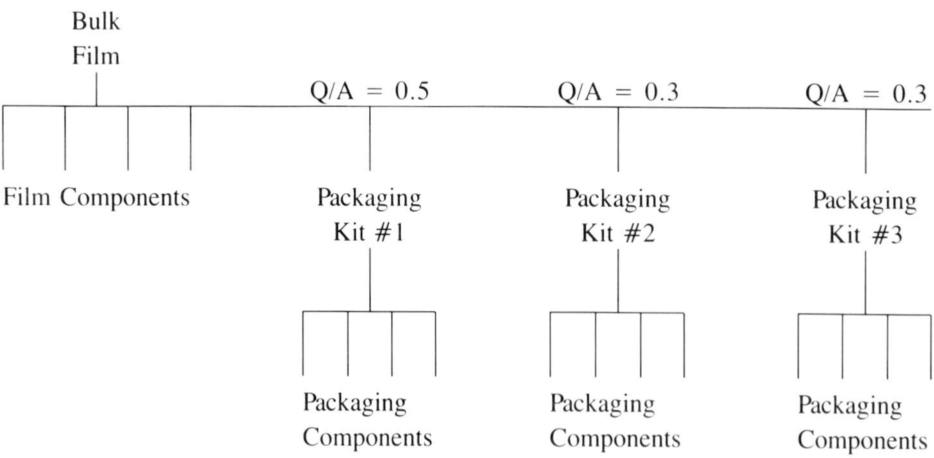

BOM for the finished, packed product is shown at the top of the figure. If the MPS is for a bulk item, say film, then requirements for the packaging will not be planned.

If the BOM is inverted, as on the lower part of the figure, this difficulty can be overcome. The packaging material is shown as a component of the basic product, with the quantity per assembly a decimal fraction based on the percent of usage of the product in individual packages compared to the total usage of the product. With the BOM inverted this way, the planning can also cover higher level components.

The percent of usage can be "hedged" a little when establishing the decimal quantity-per-assembly to use. If 10% is the long- term average usage actually experienced for a product in a certain size of packaging, then 12% placed in the BOM for this item will plan some excess packaging material. This will enable the plant to handle in any one period up to 20% more actual orders for this size package than the historical average. This is another way of overplanning, discussed in other applications in the Section, "Separating Planning From Execution", Page 54.

The decision on which of these two approaches to take depends on the accuracy of forecasts. If better forecasts can be made for the set and the individual parts, then the first approach should be used. Where the total sales of the bulk product can be predicted fairly well but the specific package size or mix of products in sets is difficult to forecast, then the second approach is better.

7. Continuous or High Volume Production — Examples of this kind of production would be home radios, automobile tires, chemicals and many textiles. The major difference with this category is that production is not in batches; some product is made in every period. The production rate of each product per day, per week or per month planned in each time period over the full horizon becomes its MPS. Products B, C, D and F on Figure 8, Page 35, are examples of this kind of MPS. Checking for capacity constraints is usually much easier for such products. Lot-sizing and lead time offsets must be handled carefully at lower levels to generate the proper flow of components.

8. Branch Warehouses — Whenever there is a distribution system consisting of company-owned branch warehouses or distributor stocks, there are alternatives which have to be weighed in creating the master schedule. One approach, sometimes called Distribution Requirements Planning, is to forecast individually the specific demands for each product at each branch warehouse. A time-phased order point is then employed to calculate planned orders to replenish each item in that warehouse. These planned order releases create demand on the central warehouse. A time-phased order point at the central warehouse, using as its requirements the branch replenishment orders, will determine demand on the factory and its production would be based on this replenishment cycle.

The second alternative is to by-pass the specific branch warehouses, forecast for each item the total customer demand on the distribution system as one figure and then use a time-phased order point comparing total forecast against total inventories, regardless of location. The replenishment orders generated are input to develop an MPS for each product. As lots are produced, specific quantities can be apportioned to each warehouse based on their current inventory level and the ratio of their usage compared to the total. This approach is sometimes called "Push" or "Allocation" systems of warehouse replenishment.

The trade-off in selecting which approach to use is dependent on desired customer service levels and costs of changing the MPS. A branch warehouse planning its own replenishment orders will attempt to optimize the inventory and distribution costs at the warehouse without considering production costs and problems. When the overall demand on all warehouses is considered, the economy of plant operations will be improved with somewhat less efficient distribution. Group forecasts will also have higher levels of accuracy than the individual forecasts for each item in the group and total inventories will be lower.

The approach selected is also dependent on the forecasting method. If items are forecast at the local level and there is no central planning, the first approach is best. If marketing forecasts of total company sales for each product are available, these should be used to create the MPS for the plant. The less reliable branch warehouse forecasts would be used only to apportion the percent of production they should receive. The latter approach must be used when total demand outstrips the capacity of the plant. Ideally, all warehouses will get an equal time-period supply of such limited products.

8. Insuring That the MPS is Realistic

This is where most failures occur in master scheduling. The objective is to make sure that the required machinery, equipment, personnel and material resources are or will be available to meet the needs of the master production schedule. The goals of insuring that capacity is adequate and raw materials are available must be met if the detailed planning is to be valid and the manufacturing process controlled well. Inaccuracies here, either in overstating or understating significantly the capability of the plant or its vendors, generate a defective plan doomed to fail. This is where all companies employing closed-loop MRP-based systems have trouble in the beginning; many have not yet solved these problems after years of operation, primarily because management teams refuse to accept constraints and do not agree on compromises. The major constraints are capacity-related and must be evaluated in one or more of the following ways:

Rough-cut Capacity Requirements Planning

The capacity requirements to support the production plan should be evaluated first in gross terms. The master production schedules, more detailed, should be kept in agreement with the production plan but they too should be tested by rough-cut capacity evaluations. This is particularly true when starting up an MRP-based system when all of the capacity implications are not well understood. This rough-cut approach is recommended to avoid long computer runs processing data that eventually proves to be inappropriate. The rough-cut test can make it almost certain that the production plan, master production schedules and detailed material plans will all be valid and in agreement.

Other merits of the rough-cut approach are that it is simple, very easy to understand and requires a minimum of data. Trade-offs among products, which must be made when the production plan or the master production schedules exceed the ability of the plant or its vendors to produce the required totals, can be examined readily. Management can ask, "What if....?" questions and study alternative plans far more easily using rough-cut data.

There are several ways to make the rough-cut evaluation; the method selected will depend to a large degree on the type of product and the processes involved. Some companies can measure the validity of their production plan using family totals of sales dollars per period based on average prices for each product. Assuming the mix of the final products will be the same or making some adjustments for changes in it, historical data from sales in previous periods when capacity was adequate will indicate whether the plan is feasible or, if it is not, what significant changes in capacity are required. This is a very gross way of evaluating the validity of plans and is most useful if there is a good way to determine the effects of mix variations on the plant's ability to produce.

Other companies use units of production (pieces, tons, gallons, average units or equivalent units). The ball-bearing industry, for instance, can use total numbers of bearings grouped in product families to determine whether plant capacity is adequate or not. For products with few levels in the bills of material and simple processes this approach works well and more detailed analyses are unnecessary.

As the products increase in complexity, the production plan and, possibly, also the MPS must be converted into hours of production necessary in major work centers. The Bill of Labor shown in Figure 10, sometimes called a resource profile, is a listing of the principal work centers showing the total hours of output necessary to produce all components of each item in the production plan or MPS. If the production plan and MPS show finished products ready to ship to customers, the BoL will include assemblies of finished products. When the MPS is stated in terms of major subassemblies or in planning modules, it will include only subassembly work and that required to fabricate all component parts.

The rough-cut CRP technique usually does no netting of materials already on hand and on order and is not time-phased to provide for labor expended in different time periods. It assumes that all the raw material and purchased items are converted into finished products in the same time periods. If the mix of products changes significantly in time periods and has a strong effect on capacity, such time-phased offsetting of hours may be necessary. **Accuracy levels of plus or minus 5% or even plus or minus 10% are adequate.** The needed data can often be obtained from cost records, manufacturing engineering data and even from supervisors who frequently know the time necessary to make parts to support a given assembly rate.

FIGURE 10
BILL OF LABOR — Family #1

Work Center	Required/1000 Units
110 Assembly	10
108 Subassembly	8
105 Drills	14
104 Turrets	28
103 Mills	9
101 Stamping	17
Suppliers	
Castings	250 Molds
Steel Sheet	500 Pounds
Fasteners	4000 Pieces

When there are many items in the production plan and MPS, even these simplified approaches involve many calculations and become tedious. A good alternative is to pick within each family of products a specific item which is typical of the family. For example, valves made in a range of sizes from ½ inch to 3 inches may be considered a family because they go through similar machining operations in the same work centers. The total time required in each work center probably does not vary much from one valve to another in this family. The bill of materials and the routings for the typical valve could be used to calculate the data for the bill of labor to determine raw and purchased materials and plant capacity requirements for all of the valves in the family.

Where a typical product is difficult to identify, a dummy product may be set up and average manufacturing times used in the bill of labor. **A high degree of precision is not necessary.** Another approach is to determine what products were made and how many standard hours were used to make them in the recent past, thus developing average hours required per unit. Where departments are organized by product line, this is very representative. Where functional departments handle a wide mix of end products, this becomes less valid; mix variations can distort the results badly.

These rough-cut evaluations can be made to highlight internal capacity constraints and also external supplier limitations. Adding specific data to the bill of labor showing the total demand that the plan places on key suppliers, as illustrated in Figure 10, will point out such external capacity constraints.

FIGURE 11
ROUGH-CUT CAPACITY PLAN IN STANDARD HOURS

Work	Families						Month #1
Centers	#1	#2	#3	#4	#5	#6, etc.	Totals
110	56						330
109							210
108	45						200
107							170
106							150
105	78						650
104	156						1450
103	50						290
102							460
101	95						1010
100							370
Suppliers							
Castings	1395 Molds						6200
Steel Sheet	2790 Pounds						11500
Nuts & Bolts	22300 Pieces						22300

Using the bill of labor, the production plan or MPS can be exploded to calculate the total standard hours required in each work center in each period. Figure 11 shows the capacity requirements for the first month of a production plan for a family of items. Most companies can do this manually or with a desk or hand calculator. If there are many items or the bill of labor is very extensive, a simple computer program may be required to do this explosion. This program would be a modification to the "Summarized Explosion" capability found in all standard computer bill-of-material-processing packages.

Figure 12 shows a summary rough-cut capacity requirements plan for several months of the production plan or master production schedule horizon. The data in the first month can be compared to existing capacity to show where work centers or suppliers are short or have excess capability compared to planned requirements. Existing capacity is most easily

FIGURE 12
SUMMARY ROUGH-CUT CAPACITY PLAN

Work Ctrs	Existing Capacity	Required Capacity/Month — Std. Hours Mo.#1	Mo.#2	Mo.#3	Mo.#4 etc.
110	320	330			
109	230	210			
108	195	200			
107	180	170			
106	170	150			
105	500	650			
104	1500	1450			
103	310	290			
102	440	460			
101	960	1010			
100	370	370			
Suppliers					
Castings	5900 Molds	6200 Molds			
Steel Sheet	12000 Lbs	11500 Lbs			
Nuts & Bolts	25000 Pcs	22300 Pcs			

determined by measuring the actual output of the workcenters in the proper units of measure for the immediately preceding month or two; this is usually called "demonstrated" capacity for obvious reasons. In the example in Figure 12, for instance, it is obvious that Workcenter 105 has not been producing nearly the amount required by the plan and also that the demands on fasteners will be increased rather significantly while casting requirements are significantly less.

Rather than comparing each month's capacity requirements to existing figures, it is better to average several months, say two or three. This eliminates the effects of the lack of netting out components already available and offsetting lead times, both of which are omitted from rough-cut capacity requirements planning. Monthly figures, of course, should not be averaged if there is a significant increase or decrease in the planned requirements in the first few months.

Spare Parts Capacity Requirements Planning

To create a bill of labor for spare parts or components furnished to affiliates is much more difficult than for end products. Spare parts often involve a huge array of items and the problem is to determine the labor requirements to produce all of them. One approach that has worked well begins with sampling historical sales of spare parts. For example, 100 spare parts orders are picked at random from those shipped over the last three months. Purchased items should, of course, be eliminated unless supplier capacity is also being evaluated. Quantities of items on the 100 orders are summarized by part number, extended by processing times in the routing of each part, sorted and summarized to get the total hours required in each work center to produce the materials on these 100 orders. An average bill of labor could then be calculated for each order. A forecast of the number of orders expected each month extended by this average would approximate the capacity requirements for all spare parts.

Another alternative is to calculate the dollars of shipments in the 100 orders sampled and determine the total hours required in each work center as before. The hours in the sample could then be divided by the value of the shipments to get the required hours in each work center per $100 of orders. Spares production would then be assumed equal to the expected sales forecast for spare parts expressed in dollars. Multiplying the hours per $100 by the hundreds of dollars in the forecast will develop the total hours required from the plant to support this level of spare parts demand. Both approaches should be tested regularly to see whether mix variations in actual spare parts orders have affected the results significantly. The data should be readjusted whenever significant changes have occurred.

Affiliate Plant Capacity Requirements Planning

Components to be furnished to an affiliate plant could be handled in a similar manner. This approach, using historical shipments to affiliates in the absence of a forecast, would give average demand from that source but significant changes in the mix of products to be made by the affiliate would have to be evaluated and the data adjusted. A better approach would be to create a bill of labor for just the components furnished by the supplier plant to each affiliate for each family of its products. Each affiliate's production plan could then be exploded through this bill of labor to determine the hours needed from the supplier plant to support it.

Comparing Required and Available Capacity

In the final analysis, the total demands of the production plan from all sources including finished products, spares and affiliates, must be compared to the ability of the plant to produce them. Rough-cut approaches have been used very effectively in getting data for such comparisons; they are very simple and thus are easy to understand. When capacity requirements are excessive or inadequate, trade-off decisions must be made by management; rough-cut totals make it easier to study alternatives caused by increases, decreases or changes to the product mix. They make the production plan a much more useful management tool to study alternate ways of laying out and operating the plant. However, rough-cut tests of the production plan cannot provide the final test of the validity of the MPS since they do not consider present levels of component and work- in-process inventories. In addition, individual work centers are likely to experience somewhat different demand from those based on the average product or assumed mix of items used in the rough- cut approaches. Unplanned demands on capacity must also be considered; these include scrap, rework, record errors (losses), new products, new methods and many others.

A much more definitive check on the MPS in the short term will come from detailed Capacity Requirements Planning (CRP). A full discussion of this topic is beyond the scope of this book (See Reference 19 in the Bibliography). This technique takes the output from MRP, in the form of open and planned orders, and uses the routings for all the manufactured parts to calculate in detail the projected work load by work center by period. This may reveal specific bottleneck or under- loaded operations, not identified by the rough-cut approach, which require changing capacity either through overtime, transfer, hiring, training, layoff, use of alternate routings or subcontracting. If the necessary adjustments to capacity cannot be made in time, the only valid alternative is to revise the MPS.

It is worth stressing that the rough-cut analysis made BEFORE MRP AND CRP ARE RUN will ensure a high degree of confidence that the MPS is feasible. This will save considerable expense by not making extensive computer runs to explode a fallacious MPS. It must also be remembered that the unplanned capacity requirements mentioned earlier will not be included in detailed CRP calculations, nor will allowances be indicated for standard or normal levels of work-in-process which make up a significant part of the load shown in such detailed calculations.

Making such a capacity plan and deciding periodically that it and the MPS "look realistic" is not enough. **Actual output must be compared to the plan to make sure that the master schedule really is and continues to be realistic.** A plan requiring 500 hours per week from a work center which seems reasonable now does not insure that 500 hours per week will continue to come out of that work center. The Input/Output Control technique, measuring the throughput of each work center, must be used to be sure that the plan is executed or that action is taken promptly to correct for significant deviations.

The final test of whether or not the MPS is realistic is, "Did it happen?". If it was realistic, the scheduled products should have been made. Data on products actually produced in each time period should be compared to the MPS; a format for doing this is shown in Figure 18. If the products were not made as planned, an analysis of the problems is needed to show if the plan was invalid or if it was poorly executed. This analysis and the actions taken as a result close the loop in the planning/control cycle. Effective control of manufacturing inventories, costs and customer service is impossible without it.

9. Planning Versus Execution

Planning and controlling manufacturing should be viewed as a two- phase activity. The planning phase involves converting firm customer orders and forecasts of future demands into material requirements and ultimately component inventories via production plans, master production schedules and material requirements planning. The second phase requires issuing assembly or finishing schedules to draw component inventories from available stocks and convert them into finished products, repair parts, and intermediate products which are to be shipped to customers.

When this is seen clearly, it becomes obvious that bills of material describing the items in the master production schedule DO NOT NEED TO BE IDENTICAL with those describing the products to be shipped to the ultimate customers. This becomes most important in companies making products with common parts or with many options available to customers for their selection. The job of the master production schedule is to initiate the procurement of sets of parts into component inventories so that they will be available in the proper amounts and mix to meet the needs of the assembly or finishing schedules which will be issued later.

Before assembly schedules are issued, planners should test the availability of all needed components and develop shortage lists from these formal system programs. Obviously, planning based on the master schedule, made well in advance of actual receipt of customer orders, will not produce exactly the sets of parts which will be needed when assembly schedules are issued later. The best that can be hoped for is to minimize the shortages and excesses in the required sets of parts.

Relation of MPS to Other Plans

The time relationships of the planning and execution phases are shown in the diagram in Figure 13. The objective of the master production schedule is to initiate procurement actions far enough in the future to have the necessary resources available when needed. It is essentially a short- to medium-range planning technique. It links the business and production plans to detailed day-to-day activities needed to support them.

As shown in Figure 13, data in the MPS in Weeks 5 — 8 link to Month 2 in the business and production plans. For the company in this example, the total manufacturing cycle is 4 weeks, so Week 5 in the MPS links to Week 1 in the MRP data for items at the bottom of the Bills of Material but is driven by Week 5 data at the top levels.

The daily priorities of work in individual work centers are driven partly by data in MRP and partly by actual performance of the plant while executing the plan. In this company, components made in Work Center 8 are scheduled to be used in final assembly two days later and then to be shipped in finished products two days after that.

FIGURE 13
PLANNING VERSUS EXECUTION

		Time Unit	Related Periods			
PLANNING	Business & Prod. Plans	Month	2			
	MPS	Week	5	6	7	8
	MRP Top	Week	5	6	7	8
	MRP Bot.	Week	1	2	3	4
EXECUTION	Wk Ctr. #8 Priority	Day	1,2,3,4,5	6 — 10	11 — 15	16 — 20
	Assembly Schedule	Day	3,4,5,6,7	8 — 12	13 — 17	18 — 22
	Shipping Schedule	Day	5,6,7,8,9	10 — 14	15 — 19	20 — 24

Assembly schedules will cause allocation or commitment of needed components to specific finished products and will reveal shortages. This will initiate further priority changes to get any components not available to meet the assembly schedules; the only alternative is to revise the assembly schedule. Thus, the two phases, planning and execution, are going on simultaneously and interacting with each other.

The master production schedule can be viewed as being made up of several phases. This was shown earlier in Figure 7, Page 33, in the section called "MPS Zones". The short range phase covering the immediate future links to the execution activities. Customer orders in-house for shipment during this period or manufacturing orders released to build inventory will define precisely what must be made. This short range segment of the MPS defines specific demands on the plant for materials and workforce, some or all of which may be in the execution phase. Changes in this segment, therefore, will initiate action notices on released and open orders which may be impossible to make. To avoid this, the idea of a "frozen" master production schedule segment is very appealing to manufacturing people but is not required to operate MRP-based closed-loop planning systems. Their role in planning must not be confused with execution activities. There is always some ability to react to desired changes in the plan; the amount of change which can be handled will be determined by the product to be built, the level of inventory in excess of other requirements and the costs involved.

The next MPS phase to consider is made up of one or more intermediate ranges. In these, the master production schedule has considerable flexibility without affecting execution activities. Rescheduling of planned orders incurs little real cost. There is also flexibility to change worker levels by hiring, transfer and retraining.

The balance of the MPS is long range planning where even more flexibility is available. In this phase, the only important constraint on the MPS is the production plan.

Separating Planning from Execution

Master production schedules must be made weeks or months in advance of the time that the resources will be needed. No matter how carefully the MPS is made nor how the bills of material associated with it are structured, the probability that exactly the right resources will be available when final execution occurs is zero. This is particularly true of materials. A perfect plan will not be made nor would it be executed perfectly if it were. The inevitable result will be that some of the needed resources will be missing when final execution is started. Most frequently the missing resource is matched sets of the correct parts for the products to be built to fill customers or warehouse replenishment orders. More sophisticated planning systems, more specific information in daily time buckets and more frequent replanning will not eliminate such shortages. **Deficiencies in planning must be overcome by actions in execution.** Two questions are relevant: What can be done to make a better, more valid plan and what can be added in cushions to minimize the shortages?

Three possible actions can be taken to improve the validity of the manufacturing plan. These are:

1. Force a match between the orders to be processed in the execution phase and the data in the master production schedule. This technique is illustrated by Figure 4, Page 24 in the earlier section headed "Sources of MPS Data." The basic assumption, easily accepted by most reasonable people, is that avoiding changes in a plan will make it a better plan more likely to be executed properly. The most common objection is that "customers won't wait for their products". The situation is illustrated best by discussing a hypothetical customer order received for delivery of twenty units of the item in Figure 4 in Week 4. This customer request is for five more units than the plan calls for delivered one week earlier. Several alternative actions are possible to meet this customer request, two of which are:

a. Allocate to him 20 of the 50 units in Week 2 originally promised to some other customer. The second customer will then have to wait for his units.

b. Allocate the 15 available units in Week 5 to the new customer plus 5 units from the 35 in Week 5 promised to some other customer (who will then wait) and complete the 20 units one week earlier than planned.

It is possible, of course, that this customer's real needs could be satisfied by giving him 15 of the 20 units in Week 5 as planned and completing his order for the balance of 5 in Week 8 when additional quantities will become available. This alternative would involve the least change in the plan, in fact no change at all. The question is whether his order states his "wants" or his "needs". Good communications and relations with customers can resolve such questions to mutual advantage.

Other possible alternatives would include increasing the MPS in Week 5 by the extra 5 units now needed or adding an additional quantity of 20 in Period 4. Both of these alternatives would involve possible extra costs and upsets which would jeopardize promised deliveries on other customer orders already in process. Some of the problems might be avoided or minimized by trading off quantities of similar items whose sales are below planned figures in the MPS and which have many common components. This would limit the changes from plan to the unique items only.

2. Cut the manufacturing cycle time. Plans spread over long horizons will obviously have many more opportunities for changes. The most important action a manufacturing company can take is to cut its lead time so that the cumulative minimum horizon of the master production schedule is greatly shortened. This subject will be discussed in more detail under the subheading, "The Future", Page 81.

3. Simplify the product line. The assumption here is that plans made for fewer items will be better since more time can be devoted to each of the remaining items planned. It is far too infrequent that companies review their product lines for deletion of slow moving and obsolete items. Unfortunately, this is done not only periodically but in a cursory way. Part of the master scheduling process should be a constant review of products brought to management's attention because sales rates have been slowing or have stopped. This can be a very rewarding activity in improving customer service as well as in meeting the other objectives of the company.

There are three alternative ways to build cushions into plans to respond more flexibly to changing demands:

1. The most effective way to provide flexibility in a plant to respond to actual orders significantly different from plan is to standardize components of the products. When various models of the products can be made with only a few unique components, significant changes in the mix can be accommodated on the majority of parts. The greatest problem in achieving such standardization is in getting the design engineering and manufacturing engineering groups to realize the benefits to manufacturing.

These benefits are usually not easily expressed in tangible costs or savings as are the materials savings and processing advantages from designing unique components for each application.The material and processing costs to machine a part from a larger diameter of bar stock or to utilize chemicals with wider ranges in the specifications are easily figured; the additional costs and difficulties of maintaining inventories of these components and insuring customer service are not easy to quantify.

The increasing use of computer assisted design (CAD) and manufacturing (CAM) programs has complicated this problem. It is now far too easy for design engineering to develop new individual designs without regard for their effect on destroying standardization. Not enough companies have educated their design engineering groups on the information in the business system on components already available, in production and even in stock which could be used in lieu of a newly designed item. The tragic failure to integrate CAD, CAM and computer assisted engineering (CAE) programs with business systems for maximum benefit to all people in the company is costing large amounts of money and effort.

2. Another way to increase the flexibility of manufacturing to respond to changing customer requirements is to add additional inventories of some components. These excess stocks are usually referred to as safety stock or buffer stock. Statistical methods for safety stock calculations have no application here. The objective is to provide additional materials to improve the company's flexibility in a marketplace. Product bills of material must be examined to determine the best place to carry excess inventories to meet potential changes in customer demand. Management policies on how much demand change should be accommodated are also required. As with any plan, the actual use of such safety stock should be reviewed periodically. If these excess materials are not being used, they should be eliminated as unnecessary. The objective must be to provide sufficient flexibility for the plant to meet changing customer demands with minimum inventories and at the same time keep plant operations relatively stable.

3. Another technique for increasing the flexibility of a plant to respond to changes in the plan is called "Overplanning". When a company's product consists of a basic unit plus customer- selection options, the forecast for the basic units can be quite good and be controlled by the production plan in total. However, the forecasts for individual, specific options that could be added to this basic unit are likely to have a much higher degree of error and may not be constrained by the production plan. Some protection against such errors is needed so that, when actual sales differ from forecast, total sales of units will not be jeopardized by shortages of options. Carrying safety stocks of components of the options, individually estimated, would result in mismatched sets, leading to large inventories and possibly poor service if the needed sets of parts were not available.

To improve the match between the MPS and the orders that can be handled, the options can be overplanned. Figure 14 shows how one company does this. An MPS has been created for the basic unit (Product #3322 shown in Figure 4). Two options which may accompany this basic unit are shown in Figure 14 with their forecast percent usage compared to the basic

FIGURE 14
OVERPLANNING OPTIONS
MAKE-TO-STOCK

Option A (60%)

Weeks	1	2	3	4	5	6	7	8	9	10	11
Master Schedule	—	35	—	—	35	—	—	40	—	—	40
Booked Orders	—	28	—	—	21	—	—	5	—	—	0
Unsold Bal.	—	—	—	—	14	—	—	35	—	—	40

Option B (10%)

Weeks	1	2	3	4	5	6	7	8	9	10	11
Master Schedule	—	6	—	—	6	—	—	8	—	—	8
Booked Orders	—	5	—	—	6	—	—	0	—	—	0
Unsold Bal.	—	—	—	—	—	—	—	8	—	—	8

unit. However, the quantity used for the MPS for each option has been increased above the average percent forecast providing an "overplan". This overplan could be based on statistical safety stock calculations or simply on judgment. Planning a little extra material for options insures that the full quantity of finished units can be shipped each period with relatively little excess inventory, resulting in less total inventory and higher service. Figure 14 illustrates overplanning for products made to stock.

New orders are booked against the MPS and an Unsold Balance line shown; this is termed "consuming the master schedule". The MRP program is not driven by the data on the line entitled "MPS" but by the sum of "Booked" and "Unsold Balance", which is the same as the MPS for the basic machine in Figure 4 but not for option "A". The option MPS is 35 in Week 2 but only 28 have been sold. However, all the basic machines scheduled prior to and in Week 2 have been sold so the extra 7 units of the option that were planned originally are no longer required by Week 2.

Several alternative ways of treating this 7 "excess" are available. In the figure, the 7 units unsold in Week 2 have been dropped and the total of 28 units booked will comprise the MPS. This would delay 7 sets of material in the option BOM. Alternatively, the 7 units could be left in the MPS and the components put into stock to help assure faster reaction to future customer demand. Another approach would be to delay the 7 units until Week 5 and increase the overplan quantity from 5 to 12 in that period. Note that this would also cause delaying messages to appear on the option's component material plans.

To decide which of these to do requires a lot of judgment. Will the demand for option "A" peak up later well above the historical average percentage? If it does, will the plant be able to handle this load or would it be better to make some components now and stock them in advance of the peak? What is the inventory investment and what useful materials may be tied up if the overplan is left in the MPS? These are not easy questions to answer. In the absence of a normal system driven by the MPS, these important questions are usually never even raised. The basic decisions of which customers get their orders and which do not when all cannot be served is all-too-often made by schedulers and expediters, not managers.

Products made to order can be handled in a different way as shown in Figure 15. This product is made to order but does not have options or accessories. Made from fairly standard raw materials, customized during production, these could be doors, windows,large electric motors or industrial fans. Products like these are extremely difficult to forecast individually,

FIGURE 15
OVERPLANNING OPTIONS
MAKE-TO-ORDER

Weeks	1	2	3	4	5	6	7	8	9	10	11	12	13
Master Schedule	—	50	—	—	50	—	—	50	—	—	50	—	—
Overplan	—	—	—	—	—	—	—	15	—	—	—	—	—
Booked Orders	—	50	—	—	35	—	—	10	—	—	0	—	—
Un-committed	—	—	—	—	15	—	—	55	—	—	50	—	—

so forecasts for product classes or families are provided. If the "stacked" lead time to procure materials and make the item is less than the quoted lead time to customers there is no problem. However, if it is longer, materials must be procured and early stages of manufacture completed based on forecasts used to develop the MPS. Forecasts are sure to be wrong, customer orders will not match the MPS and shortages will plague production; high inventories and poor customer service will result.

Overplanning can be used here also to minimize this as shown in Figure 15. Here a family bill of materials has been used beyond the customer order horizon to translate the MPS into purchased material requirements. An overplan quantity in the MPS in the first time period beyond the stacked internal manufacturing cycle time (in this example 7 weeks) will provide additional sets of purchased items. The overplan shown in Period 8 in Figure 15 will provide extra materials necessary to react quickly when actual demand varies from forecast. If sales do not materialize, keeping the overplan always in the same relative period in the future will limit the increase in the total inventory to the extra raw and purchased materials and will not consume capacity in the plant. When extra items are sold, the added quantities of components needed are brought to completion and additional overplan added, if capacity is available to produce them.

The technique of overplanning the MPS is very effective in providing protection against differences between demand and planned amounts. It is extremely powerful in helping execute the plan since it overplans items in MATCHED SETS based on bills of material, rather than via safety stock on each item; the latter approach rarely gives balanced inventories. It is also a powerful tool for management. The overplan is highly visible, can be costed easily and trade-off alternatives can be considered as conditions change. This is obviously impossible with safety stock applied to each component or raw material individually.

It is important that management set reasonable limits of flexibility in meeting changing customer demand. The use of such words as "always" and "never" being out of stock or being unable to deliver products should be avoided. The actual costs of attempting to achieve such goals can be ridiculously high. Compromises between the normal wish of marketing people to serve all customer needs as they arise and the desire of manufacturing people to have a stable plan are not easy to make. As has been mentioned, specific data on costs involved and extra inventories required for such flexibility are difficult to get, will never be precise and in many cases cannot be quantified at all. The MPS should represent managements' best collective judgment on how they would like the business to be run. There is no other way such judgments can be expressed or policies implemented.

In the literature and discussions of master production scheduling in the past, the word "fence" has been used frequently. Such fences have been suggested as ways to mark periods of time which were discussed earlier in the Section "MPS Zones", Page 33. Much of the discussion of fences, however, focused on the first time zone when planning and execution are interacting closely. The suggestion was made frequently that this section of the MPS be "frozen" to keep a stable plan in this period on the assumption (usually fallacious) that neither the plant nor its suppliers could deviate from actions being taken under present plans.

This was the same as saying to marketing people, "If we haven't planned it, you can't get it." and also saying to manufacturing, "If we have planned it you will make it, whether we still need it or not". When these concepts are expressed this way it becomes clear immediately how patently ridiculous the approach of freezing a portion of the master production schedule becomes. The effectiveness of expediting actions taken practically every day in the real world of manufacturing proves conclusively that plants and their suppliers are far more flexible than these assumptions would conclude.

Rather than arguing about the location of a time fence and the amount of change permissible within such a fence if any, it is far better to make every attempt to improve the validity of the master production schedule as discussed earlier in this section and to provide cushions of extra inventory in safety stocks or overplanned quantities to make it possible to react to changes in actual demand from the planned quantities. A technique called "Allocations", discussed in detail in Reference 19 in the Bibliography, can be provided in the formal computer planning system to determine if there are any shortages to build any specific product desired.

This technique provides the first and a very vital step in the execution process. The detailed schedule of customer orders to be completed or warehouse replenishment orders to be shipped this week can be tested by means of the allocation program to detect existing shortages of components utilizing the formal system rather than physical staging of materials. Specific shortages can be identified and investigations made to determine the possibility of overcoming them in time to complete the orders on schedule. **It does not matter whether or not the orders being tested for availability of components are similar to items originally planned in the master production schedule.**

The allocation process actually replaces the planning process driven by the front end of the master production schedule. The basic procedure is:

1. Forget what was planned in the MPS.
2. Decide what is really desired to be made today or this week.
3. Determine what shortages might prevent this.
4. Investigate the problems of overcoming these shortages.
5. Reschedule later items for which components cannot be obtained in time.

As stated at the beginning of this section, manufacturing planning and control is a two-phased process. The planning phase, no matter how soundly developed and no matter how frequently revised, cannot insure that all components will be available for manufacture of the products actually needed for customer and warehouse demands. Plans can be made more valid by forcing customer orders to fit master production schedule quantities, cutting manufacturing cycle times or reducing the number of products to be planned. They can be protected against shortages by the addition of safety stocks and overplanned quantities in the MPS plus a maximum use of common standard components. The fact remains, however, that customer orders desired will be different from customer orders planned and shortages will be present. Far better than freezing the plan is a flat out attempt to overcome the shortages. The fence in the master production schedule defining the first segment or zone consequently should be viewed not as a frozen portion of a plan but rather as a time frame within which the planning phase will be abandoned and the execution phase will take over.

10. The Production/Delivery Ratio

An important fact in any business is the relationship between the total time to manufacture products, including procuring the necessary materials, and the time allowed by the customer for delivery after his order has been received. The smaller this ratio, the more materials will have to be bought and manufactured based on forecasts and plans; the higher this ratio the more work can be done on products built to definitive orders after receipt from the customer.

Figure 16 summarizes the relationships between customer allowed times and the types of production which can be employed. If the ratio exceeds 1, then materials can be both procured and manufactured into products and a true make-to- order situation prevails.

FIGURE 16
PRODUCTION VERSUS DELIVERY CYCLES

Customer Allowed Time	Activities Driven by Forecasts and Orders
6 Months	——— To Customer Order ——— Buy-Fabrication Operations-Assemble-Test-Pack Make-to-Order
1 Week	——— To Forecast ——— + ———To Customer Order——— Buy-Stock-Fab. Opns.-Stock- + -Asmbl.-Test-Pack Assemble-to-Order
1 Day	——— To Forecast ——— Buy-Stock-Fab. Opns.-Stock-Asmbl.-Test-Pack-Stock Made-to-Stock

Even in this situation, many factors can introduce upsets in plans and processing. A rash of engineering changes to correct unexpected problems, changes by customers in quantities ordered or dates of delivery and failure of the plant or its suppliers to produce the necessary components on time can all dictate the need for revising the plan. Building to inventory based upon long range plans or forecasts, however, will always be a more uncertain process than building to customers orders. A later section, "The Future", Page 81, will contain a further discussion of the importance of cutting manufacturing cycle times.

11. MAINTENANCE OF THE MPS

All significant changes to the MPS should be approved at high levels of management. As will be discussed in the next section, "Uses of the MPS", Page 65, the company's game plan stated by the MPS directly affects profitability, customer service and inventory levels, the three basic objectives of all companies.

The MPS must be changed to suit several conditions, some of them normal operating events and some unusual or extreme activities. As shown in "The MPS Format" Figure 8, Page 35, there should be no past due time bucket. It is mandatory to change an MPS when planned quantities are not actually built. This may result from a previously overstated MPS, vendor falldown, machine breakdown, faulty material or other cause. If, for whatever reason, the products in the MPS are not all built, some customer order deliveries will be jeopardized or some products could go out of stock. Allowing past due buckets in the MPS will not help; this will simply drive all of the material planning system into a behind-schedule condition. Actually it is a fallacy — products at the MPS level cannot and will not be produced in the past.

Dumping the past due into the first few periods or "front- ending", does not solve the problem. MRP-based systems are powerful in providing valid priorities — showing which orders are really needed first. They lose this power if the MPS is badly front-ended. Such a system can tell a supervisor that there is a 20- week load of past due work; it cannot answer the real question, "What's the next job I should work on?"

Under one circumstance it is proper to overstate the first time bucket. This occurs when the overdue products are essentially complete except for a few missing purchased components or require only testing or packaging which can be accomplished with very little labor. The MPS will still be valid, and so will the priorities on missing materials, if there is adequate capacity not only to finish items that are almost all done but also to complete those that are not yet started. This is an extremely difficult decision to make and it is too easy to be optimistic. Experienced people recognize the danger of believing assembly will catch-up — they have seen it happen so rarely.

The MPS must also change when needed material cannot be obtained in time. Specific items can be identified by MRP as falling behind schedule, usually due to capacity limitations but often because of other problems. This does not mean that every schedule slippage should force a change in the MPS. Delay in receiving a purchased item several levels down in the bill of material may or may not affect the MPS. Manufacturing lead times at each level in bills of material contain a substantial amount of queue (or waiting time) at each work center. These queues can be "compressed" for urgently needed orders; the higher the priority the order receives in any work center, the shorter the time it is allowed to sit there in queue. Higher priority on delayed orders coupled with adequate capacity to handle all needed orders makes it possible to **get back on schedule and avoid changing the MPS.**

Every effort should be made to follow the master production schedules whenever possible, making priority and capacity changes within the plant to get late work back on schedule. If, however, this cannot be accomplished, the MPS MUST BE CHANGED. Revising the MPS realigns the priorities of all related items in each bill of materials to the one behind schedule. This, in turn, frees up capacity and materials that can then be used for other high priority items. Failure to reschedule could result in wasted capacity with excess inventories of most components, shortages of a few, inability to build and ship the right products and, hence, poor customer service. The worst of both worlds is having high inventory and poor customer service, the inevitable result of an unrealistic MPS.

Changing market conditions dictate changes in the MPS. Sudden changes require careful analysis to determine whether or not it is realistic to change the master production schedule in the short range. There is consideralble near-term inertia in most manufacturing operations; it gets very expensive to increase or decrease production sharply and quickly. Simply changing numbers in the master schedule will have little real effect on production and may upset plant operation dramatically, generating excessive costs with little benefit to customer service.

The master schedule in the short term should be changed only for compelling reasons and only after enough study to make sure that the revised plan can be carried out. The MPS should also be updated at least monthly for the effects of significant forecast errors. However, their effects on the MPS should be checked first; changes should not be made automatically. They should be introduced in the intermediate and long-range future whenever possible; only if necessary and feasible should changes be made in the short-term.

A very useful technique for evaluating changes in the master production schedule is called "Requirements Alteration". For a detailed discussion of this, see Reference 19 in the Bibliography. This can be employed as a simulation technique to study the effect of changes. It also provides a good approximation of net-change MRP for changes to the MPS. This technique accepts a change to one portion of the master production schedule and shows the effects of this change only through all levels in the bills of material to highlight specific material shortages or excesses this may create. Exception conditons are flagged on only those items affected by each change. It is a very useful technique to answer the sales department's questions on a new, large customer order, "When can we get it in the schedule?" or, "If we put this in when the customer wants it, what other orders will be affected?"

Many companies, in the early stages of using the MPS, wonder how the available knowledgeable people will be able to cope with the details and handle all the changes. The question to answer, however, is not, "How will people cope?" but "What procedures should they follow and what help do they need so that they can cope?" **There is no substitute for a well-maintained, up-to-date, realistic MPS.**

12. USES OF THE MPS

Companies are now using the MPS and its associated MRP programs in many different ways and new uses are being developed as more people gain experience with master scheduling. The best of present practices will be discussed here.

Resource Planning

This was covered in detail in the section "Insuring That the MPS is Realistic", starting on Page 45. One of the most important uses of the MPS is to link the Business and Production Plans with the day-to-day schedules. This insures that all plans are integrated and support each other.

Material Planning

Probably the best known use of the master production schedule is to provide the input to MRP programs for material planning and control. An example of this is shown in Figure 17, where the MPS is exploded through 3 levels of a bill of materials and the material plans for one item at each level are illustrated considering current inventory levels, open replenishment orders, lead times and lot-sizing. Note that no safety stock is planned.

All the component material plans are linked via the BOM to the MPS and are developed to support it. Inventory and open order balances are adjusted, engineering design and MPS changes are introduced and adjustments made to inventory or open order balances as they occur. The material plans are updated at intervals (weekly — called regeneration — or more frequently by net-change) and MRP keeps the need dates of open orders valid and revises quantities and dates of planned orders. The initiating and driving element for material planning is the MPS.

Contrast this with applying order points, the other technique for replenishing inventories. Order points are calculated for each part, usually based on its historical usage, ignoring the way raw materials, parts and assemblies are related in bills of material. Customer orders are then entered without regard to the load implications and replacement orders for material are triggered as each part's inventory drops to its order point level. The priority of each replacement order is established by the due date assigned when it is released; the technique is incapable of revising it. It cannot replan; it is reactive only, influenced by events after they occur. It provides no forward visibility of future orders.

Capacity Planning

The MPS also provides the basic input for capacity planning programs. The term "Capacity" as used here measures a plant's capability to make the desired total of product output. It encompasses the workforce, machines, equipment, tooling and vendor support. Having enough capacity to support the manufacturing plan is the only way to insure that products will be made when scheduled and that customer orders are delivered as promised. Actual and planned capacity levels should be compared and action taken to correct falldowns to insure that plant output schedules and incoming material flows are in balance and will support the MPS.

FIGURE 17
MPS AND MRP

				Master Production Schedule					
Week No.		40	41	42	43	44	45	46	47
Will Make			20		30		25		35
				Final Assembly Components					
Require			20		30		25		35
Have Now	10								
Will Get			10						
Need					30		25		35
Start				30		25		35	
				Subassembly Component					
Require				30		25		35	
Have Now									
Will Get				30					
Need						25		35	
Start				25		35			
				Purchased Component					
Require				25		35			
Have Now	40								
Will Get									
Need						20			
Start		100							

Resource planning is needed to determine capacity required to meet the long-range needs of the future. The production plan, extending over the long term and interpreted via bills of labor for typical products (See Figure 10, Page 46) provides the basic data for such planning. Risk analysis based on upper and lower limits of demand forecasts improves the planning. With sound planning, new plants and equipment can be ready to operate when they are needed. Contrast this with waiting until the present facilities are overloaded, hugh backlogs of customer orders exist and the plant must be expanded on a crash basis. Such new capacity too often becomes available only after business has again slackened and it cannot be utilized economically.

The importance of risk analysis and flexibility planning cannot be over-emphasized. New machines are rarely available until a year or more after the need is identified and must often be run for another 5 years to be fully amortized. Product designs, sales volumes and mix can change dramatically during these horizons. These potential changes must be factored into any long-range capacity plans and contingency plans made to shorten reaction times.

Making Customer Delivery Promises

The MPS simplifies dramatically the job of making customer delivery promises. Current customer orders can be allocated against a plan showing what, when and how much is going to be built, as was shown earlier in Figure 4, Page 24. This company, in addition to the basic machine shown in Figure 4, also provides options which customers can select to suit their applications. Data for two of the options are shown in Figure 14, Page 57. The use of such data in making delivery promises is obvious. More will be said about this later in the Section, "Problems with the MPS," Page 74.

The use of the MPS for making delivery promises can help resolve many conflicts that can be handled properly only by the management team. If capacity cannot be increased to handle an additional order, the only alternative to delaying the order is to divert into a later period another order already scheduled, to free up needed materials and capacity for this new order. With a sound MPS properly executed valid customer delivery promises can be made by sales or marketing personnel directly, consulting with manufacturing only when significant changes are involved. Answering customer inquiries on delivery promises and the status of their orders is simple and straightforward; higher levels of management need get involved only with exceptional cases. It becomes possible to notify a customer in advance if delivery cannot be made as promised with a good MPS supported by a sound well-managed system. Over 98% on-time delivery performance has been achieved consistently for very large, complex machines requiring six to nine months to produce.

Budgeting

An MPS backed by MRP programs provides vital input for manufacturing budgets. Finished goods inventory budgets stem from the finished product build plan minus the shipment forecast. The MRP net, time-phased explosion, driven by the MPS, projects planned levels of finished component and raw material inventories. MRP shows "Projected Available" data, as does the time-phased order point technique (See Figure 5, Page 27), which can be converted into an "Ideal" budget by multiplying the projected available balances by the standard cost. A realistic budget would, of course, be higher since the MRP plan undoubtedly will not be perfect, nor will it be executed perfectly. The difference between ideal and realistic will measure how sound the plan is and how well the organization as a whole, not just manufacturing, executes it.

Open manufacturing orders and planned orders indicate work-in- process inventory levels and can be used to project direct and indirect labor budgets, plus those for many supplies. Using firm and planned orders in MRP, purchased material commitments and payables can be budgeted by time period for cash flow requirements. As with inventory budgets, realistic figures will be higher than the ideal levels projected by the system in the current plan.

Capacity planning and control can also provide workforce requirements easily. Budgets for direct labor can be based on these data instead of detailed orders in MRP. Supporting expenses for indirect labor, supplies, employee benefits and the like, can also be related to this definitive picture of needs for people averaged over the planning horizon. The Employee Relations Department can use such data in planning hiring, training and transfer programs.

Developing plans from the MPS for expansion of fixed capital in plant and equipment was described in the Section on "The MPS Horizon", Page 31. These plans can be converted to dollars so that their financial impact can be evaluated and plans made to obtain the necessary funds on the most favorable basis. Relating all the budgets to each other and to the operating plans via the master production schedule allows significant changes in the MPS or operating programs to be reflected and measured through the budgeting system. This is a control badly needed in today's environment. Few companies have it and those that do find it powerful.

Profit Planning

Closely allied to budgeting is profit planning. The MPS, worked down the bills of material by MRP, is converted into purchased material and capacity needs; looking upward, it can be converted into the projected cost of goods sold. The MPS, backing up the sales plan, shows how the sales income will be generated.

Allowing for overhead costs, a picture of the projected profit per period can be made. The advantage of doing this through the MPS is that the effects on profits of major changes in product mix or production rates can be evaluated rigorously. The profit plan will then be current, reflecting the latest conditions in both the market place and plant.

Monitoring Factory Performance

Most factories and the people who run then are not measured on performance to the master production schedule. They are measured on performance against items in expense budgets such as setup time, machine utilization, labor efficiency and cost of supplies. These measures, although valid, are relatively unimportant from an overall company standpoint. The most significant measures are **producing the total throughput necessary and adherence to schedule.** Planning based on a master production schedule and measuring actual performance against plan, as is done in Figure 18, will give a much better handle on the total efficiency of the plant. The traditional measures focus on trivia. The MPS should be viewed as a contract among sales, manufacturing, engineering and finance and performance of all these groups must be measured to insure that this contract is honored.

FIGURE 18
COMPARING ACTUAL PRODUCTION WITH MPS

			Week					
		Roll Over	23	24	25	26	June	Roll Over
12 A 3	MPS		50	—	50	—	100	
	Actual	—	48	—	52	—	100	—
12 B 4	MPS		610	610	610	610	2440	
	Actual	(10)	603	601	610	625	2439	(1)
12 C 2	MPS		340	360	380	400	1480	
	Actual	(12)	342	355	373	400	1470	(10)
12 D 3	MPS		180	180	180	180	720	
	Actual	5	185	176	178	180	719	(1)
12 E 4	MPS		15	—	—	—	15	
	Actual	—	—	15	—	—	15	—
12 F 1	MPS		205	205	205	205	820	
	Actual	8	206	202	203	207	818	(2)
12 Family								
	Planned		1400	1355	1425	1395	5575	
	Actual	(9)	1384	1349	1416	1412	5561	(14)
Production Plan							5600	

Scheduling Engineering

Many products need a large amount of custom engineering before they are made. Getting information on them from the engineering department in the sequence needed by manufacturing is usually difficult. Engineers approach the design of a product exactly opposite to the way it is manufactured. They start from the end item and break it down through assemblies and subassemblies to the purchased items and raw material. Material control, however, needs to know requirements for purchased parts and raw material first; information on higher level parts can come later.

An MPS specifically stating when a given product will be built can be analyzed to show when engineering data are needed. Partial releases of design details will permit material procurement to begin without waiting until the whole design job is finished. Obviously, the long lead time items should be designed and released first; These will control the actual shipment date. Working to target dates related to lead times to procure and manufacture components, engineers can avoid unnecessary delays in starting work because they "didn't know it was needed yet". They might even lose their reputation as the "greatest consumers of lead time known to man".

One company is using the MPS to measure engineering on work output. Every customer order needs some engineering design work. The designers and draftsmen are viewed the same as starting manufacturing operations and must release each week the volume of work needed to keep the plant functioning at its required output level. Controls are established on the actual volume of work released by the engineering department each week. The usual syndrome of taking too long on engineering and having too little time left for manufacturing is not evident in this company.

Coordinating Major Departments

"Master scheduling provides the basis for resolving the inevitable conflicts between management functions because it becomes a contract between them". "The master production schedule becomes manufacturing's commitment to marketing and marketing's commitment to customer". "The master production schedule is a plan that reconciles and balances demand (quantity and priority) and capacity". "It is not only practical, but mandatory, in order to achieve simultaneously the objectives of high service, low inventory and high productivity to start any production and inventory control systen with a master production schedule and tie material and component quantity, priority and detailed capacity controls to it".

These quotes are from two of the early papers on the subject of master scheduling, both authored by Romeyn Everdell (References 8 and 9 in the Bibliography). He has captured in these quotes the essence of the primary objective of master scheduling, which is to serve as a game plan for the company, a plan to which all functions of the company subscribe and work to implement. Probably the most important use of the master production schedule is in developing this common game plan to be used by all departments of a company.

Most companies operate on several different strategies at the same time. Marketing is trying to develop ways to sell the maximum amount of product. Manufacturing is concerned with reducing costs and improving efficiency. Engineering is busy designing new products and processes and improving the existing ones. Finance is precoccupied with profit planning, cash flow, capital needs and the state of the order backlog and wondering why the company plans hardly ever materialize.

Each is fighting a different battle within the company; there is no coordinated attack on competition and the overall problems of the business. As Pogo said, "We have met the enemy and he is us"; this describes operations in too many companies. Properly made, the MPS provides one plan agreed to by all departments as the best way to run the company. Each department's goals and objectives are then dovetailed into this plan.

Extending the use of MRP from an order-launching technique to one of maintaining valid priorities on open replenishment orders and providing input data to capacity planning shows the complete inter-dependency of capacity and priority, how material ordering and people/machine planning must be linked. Statistical order point approaches can develop no interlocking of the efforts of marketing, manufacturing, engineering and finance. The order point system, driven from historical parts usage or at best a one-time annual explosion of the forecast, has no straightforward way to react to the latest marketing intelligence in procuring materials at the right time.

The order point approach cannot keep need dates on released orders valid; the oldest technique in manufactuirng control, expediting, is needed to get the proper orders shipped on time. When planning for the necessary labor force and machinery is based on backlogs of work and is not influenced by the sales forecast, the proper balance between available and needed resources cannot be obtained. Marketing usually has little interest in limitations of plant capacity. With fragmented systems, the financial people must use their own versions of black magic to create budgets, profits plans and inventory targets. Hence each department has its own strategies, fights its own wars and works toward its own limited goals because there are no common plans to work together to achieve the overall company objectives.

The MPS is the tool to integrate these factions. A realistic master plan can be developed for any company and approved by marketing, manufacturing, finance, and engineering considering existing limitations in the company's resources. Actions can be planned in each department to support the overall plan and changes to plan agreed upon and implemented in timely fashion by the respective departments. The master production schedule provides this master plan.

Having one game plan, measuring performance against that plan and working to make it happen is the only way to coordinate the activities of diverse groups in a manufactuing company. Companies doing this well are seeing dramatic improvements not only in the degree of coordination and cooperation that exists among all their major groups but also in profits, return on investment and customer service. Working together to solve problems and achieve a common goal is mandatory for success; the master production schedule provides the means to do this.

13. Problems With the MPS

Master scheduling is the most mismanaged technique in industry today. Far too many companies run without an MPS but, even where one exists, the desire of top management and marketing people to make it a "wish list" is practically irresistable. A realistic MPS is extremely difficult to maintain. Every company that now has one has gone through agonies to get it and to keep it valid. These major problems occur frequently:

Invalid Input Data

The inputs to the master production schedule were listed and discussed in the Section, "Sources of MPS Data", Page 22. Omissions of products or parts having a significant demand total will result in the MPS being badly understated. Errors in the data used will have significant effects on the validity of the MPS. Grossly inaccurate forecasts or work content data, for example, may allow creation of an apparently feasible MPS; executing the plan, however, won't develop adequate production rates to match the company's actual sales. Errors in finished goods inventory data, such as on-hand balances and replenishment order quantities and dates, will develop material excesses and deficiencies or excessive rescheduling will result as errors are discovered and corrected.

All of the data used to create the MPS must be analyzed critically to reduce errors. Measurement techniques designed to identify errors in the data must be part of any well-run MPS. The use of tracking signals for forecasting and of cycle counting for inventory record accuracy measurements help to highlight invalid data easily, permitting identification and elimination of causes of errors and lead to the development of dependable, high levels of accuracy.

Finishing Schedule Versus MPS

Some companies use their assembly schedules as the MPS. This assumes that all areas of the plant will run in direct support of the assembly area. This is frequently not the best way to operate fabrication areas in a plant and may even be impractical. A product like chain saws with seasonal demand may require highly-skilled component fabrication personnel difficult to hire and train to be productive whereas the assembly people could be low-skilled, easily obtained and trained. The assembly plan could follow the seasonal sales curve closely, using housewives, summer help and selective overtime. Skilled fabrication people cannot be hired and laid off to suit this curve, however, so the MPS is laid out to develop level-load requirements for the fabrication areas.

This type of MPS really plans for sets of machined parts to be stocked; they can be assembled later as sales require. During the low sales months, the fabrication area will be building inventories of components and the assembly area will be building inventories of finished goods and subassemblies but at a slower rate. During the high sales months, the fabrication rate will be held constant but the assembly area will increase its output rate, supported by the excess inventories of components. Excess inventories of finished goods and sub-assemblies will be available in periods when sales exceed the assembly rate.

This example shows clearly the difference between the final assembly schedule and the MPS for seasonal production. All companies, not only those with seasonal sales, should separate the MPS from the assembly or finishing schedule. As stated in the section "Objectives of Master Scheduling", Page 21, the role of the MPS is to provide components, often at a lower level than the finished item shippable to a customer. A good example of this is the production of chemicals modified, tinted or packaged to make a large number of finished items. The MPS should plan for manufacture of the bulk intermediate chemical; The finishing schedule should produce the end products.

Another example is automobile assembly where the MPS plans making engines, chassis, transmissions, bodies and other modules over the relatively long lead times involved. The individual autos are assembled at a planned rate to suit the option choices of the customer or dealer who ordered them. The MPS plans over a long horizon; the assembly schedule covers a few days or weeks at most. The MPS uses bills of material for components (engines, chassis, air conditioning, etc.); the assembly schedule deals with the final car.

Overstated MPS

When the country's economy is booming and demand for a company's products is high, there is an irresistable urge to overstate the master production schedule. This can be done in a number of ways. First, having a large quantity "past due" overstates the true requirements. As discussed in the section "Maintenance of the MPS", Page 63, nothing can be made yesterday. All past due quantities in the master schedule must be eliminated before the MPS can be realistic. Too often people do this by moving all the past due into the first two or three time periods; then all these are grossly overstated. This "front-ending" is as bad as having past due quantities. Only by facing up to actual conditions and making the MPS data valid throughout its horizon will the control system be able to do its job.

Overstated master production schedules may generate problems which show up only on components at lower levels in the bills of material. The MPS may look level and reasonable but lower-level parts show big backlogs of past due orders. This is a clear indication of a capacity constraint that was not recognized when the MPS was set. Increasing the capacity or reducing the master production schedule to relieve these backlogs are the only valid alternative solutions to this problem. Only then will MRP be able to assign realistic priorities for the guidance of supervisors and vendors.

There is a fine line between overstating and overplanning the MPS. Overplanning is developed and managed to avoid capacity constraints and not distort true priorities. Overstating lumps numbers into periods without regard to capacity limitations and hence destroys valid priorities.

Nervousness of the Plan

Master production schedules must recognize the existence of inertia in changing production rates which exists in practically every plant. It must also recognize that most plants can produce well only at a reasonably level rate. It is the rare plant that has the ability to make significant changes in production rates quickly. This means that master production schedules must be reasonably stable, at least as far as total hours demanded from the plant. Tradeoffs can be made among products running through the same work centers or over the same equipment if materials are available. The rough-cut capacity planning techique discussed in the Section "Insuring That the MPS is Realistic", Page 45, can be used to make such tradeoffs practical. Excessive nervousness in the MPS wastes both material and capacity, adds cost and precludes good customer service.

Safety stock at the master production schedule level can limit nervousness in the MPS as was discussed in the section, "Separating Planning from Execution", Page 54. The time-phased order point, Figure 5, Page 27, uses a forecast of demand to create planned orders to serve as input to the MPS. The actual demand in any period will always differ from the forecast. If it is greater, the system will indicate that some planned orders will be needed earlier. One period later the actual demand will probably be less than the forecast, returning the planned orders to their original position. An example of this was given in the earlier section, "Sources of MPS Data", Page 28.

Many might assume that planned safety stocks would dampen such movement but they cannot because the system treats them as inviolate. The time-phased order point program will not allow the safety stock to be automatically consumed when demand exceeds forecast and replaced when it is less; it acts to protect it by rescheduling planned orders. Planned safety stock is unable to buffer; it does nothing to keep the variability of demand from affecting the MPS beyond the firm orders issued.

An individual or team managing the MPS can, of course, ignore such variability and refuse to alter the data in the MPS file. Companies with many hundreds or thousands of items, however, may prefer to make the MPS at the forecast level rather than using planned orders from a time-phased order point program. Such an approach will suffer from extreme nervousness caused by actual demand varying from forecast.

A technique that can be used to solve this problem is the firm planned order. This is a replenishment order not yet released but coded specifically so that the system will not move it between time periods like it will a normal planned order. Unlike a firm order, it is exploded to develop requirements on lower level components. When planned orders in the near future in a time-phased order point program are coded as firm, actual demand variability will not cause the apparent need to change the MPS. A periodic review or a tracking signal is needed to determine when the actual demand differs significantly or consistently enough to require a change in firm planned order scheduling and in the MPS. The firm planned order has other uses in helping validate the MPS. Reference 20 in the Bibliography contains a more complete discussion of these.

Level MPS Versus Level Work Center Loads

Levelling the MPS is necessary but not sufficient to insure level workloads in the work centers. As the MPS is exploded through MRP, each level is lot-sized and batches of the same part from different orders will combine in specific time periods. This results in erratic demands at lower levels of the BOM which causes erratic loads on people and machines. Input/Output control helps to solve this problem, smoothing out the peaks and valleys of suggested order releases and feeding a level rate of work into work centers regardless of the specific time-period requirements developed by the MRP program. If this level input matches the average requirements of the MPS, the work centers will be able to handle the total load and the MPS will still be valid. If this is not true, overloaded work centers will fall behind schedule and the products in the MPS will not be made when planned.

Let The Computer Do It

Companies with many stocked finished products have applied statistical forecasting and computerized order point techniques quite successfully. When they develop and apply time-phased, MRP-based systems to control components, they attempt to link order points and MRP directly in the computer. They use time- phased order points to develop planned orders for products over the MPS horizon and these become the MPS driving the MRP program. Computer software packages aid and abet this practice, since many are programmed in this way.

This may cause no trouble when capacity is adequate but this approach cannot work over the long pull. It ignores the capacity implications and the need to evaluate the MPS before it is exploded. There must be a manual management interface between computer programs for finished good planning and those for component parts. The only exception to this that can be effective is the firm planned order discussed in Paragraph 4 in this section under the title "Nervousness of the Plan".

14. Organization

A realistic master production schedule, supported by a complete, integrated planning and control system is mandatory for any company desiring to be a world-class competitor. The MPS provides the company's game plan, where corporate strategies, policies and objectives are translated into a detailed operating plan. One of the major benefits of the process of creating the MPS is the higher degree of cooperation that can be achieved among all departments in a company, focusing their attention on common objectives and insuring that their detailed actions support this plan.

Top Management

The MPS provides a focal point for the whole organization, concentrating the attention of all top-level managers on a unifying strategy so that their departments' tactics can be developed to support it. It is a top management "tool" rather than the province of any one organization group. It must reflect the working compromises developed to reconcile the opposing and independent interests of these groups. Generally management's role is defined as setting objectives, developing plans, assigning responsibility for planning and execution, allocating resources to operate the business, measuring performance against plans and taking corrective action to achieve the objectives set originally.

Two problems influence the setting of the proper objectives: they are established without the necessary facts on which to base correct decisions or some objectives which should be established are not stated. To illustrate the former, many managers set inventory turnover goals in relation to industry average figures published by trade associations. This makes two assumptions: first, that operations of all companies in the group are comparable and second, that the other companies are managing their operations properly. Both of these assumptions are highly questionable. What's needed is some way to determine "par for the course". This is provided by a full, integrated system operated by managers who really understand their business. Typical of objectives which are not set are the improvement of the accuracy of records and a reduction in manufacturing cycle times. Failure to make either of these an active, ongoing objective delays actions which must be taken before companies can achieve sound performance.

Top management's role in developing and utilizing the MPS should include:

1. Understanding its functions. These are covered in detail under the earlier section "Objectives", Page 21.

2. Setting policies and guidelines for all people making detailed decisions in the planning and execution processes. These are unique to each company and represent the desires of management in operating their business. Many factors relevent to these were covered in the earlier section entitled "Strategic Planning", Page 8.

3. Resolving conflicts when differences arise among managers at lower levels on how

operations should be conducted. These are inevitable; managers focusing on their own functions and problems will have extreme differences of opinion on how operations should be conducted to resolve these.

4. Insuring planning is realistic. This is probably the most difficult of all tasks for top management. There is an irresistable urge to plan optimistically and to take orders as they come regardless of the capabilities of the facilities to support the needed production. Coupled with the natural desire to keep the workforce lean and to keep plant and equipment utilization at high levels, the result is inevitably overloading the MPS. As discussed earlier in the section "Problems With The MPS", Page 74, this is probably the most troublesome of all actions management can tolerate. The consistent use of a valid set of plans is the hallmark of competent, professional management who know how manufacturing must be operated.

5. Reviewing the MPS regularly and vigorously. This set of numbers provides management's means for authorizing the utilization of resources of the company. It provides their best "handle" on the business. Its development and use provide the means whereby high level decisions can be converted into low level activities which support them. Thus the whole management team is working to the same game plan.

Top management must also define the primary roles of each major organizational group. To operate a manufacturing business the way it ought to be, this will require redefining and challenging some long-held convictions. The team must be converted from a group of all-stars expert in their own functions and concerned only with their departments' performance into an effective working team. Full treatment of this subject is beyond the scope of this book but a few of the more inportant considerations will be highlighted in the following paragraphs.

Design Engineering

This function has long been identified with the technical and functional design of products. While some close integration of their activities with marketing has been achieved, close cooperation with manufacturing has been conspicuous in its absence. In addition to developing functioning products which meet the customer's needs, engineering's primary role must be enlarged to include the presentation of detailed information and properly structured bills of material and the development of products which fit the manufacturing facilities of the company. Engineering is probably the outstanding example of an all-star who must be made into a team player.

Marketing

Traditionally, marketing's role has been to develop an understanding of the customer's wants in both product design and in quantities. Just as many companies are now improving operations enormously by closer cooperation with suppliers, a better understanding between a company and its customers can lead to dramatic benefits. Marketing's primary role should be to provide the intelligence of the company in the marketplace of its customers. Such intelligence must include early warnings of changes in customers' real requirements as well as communication of the customer's real needs as contrasted to his wants. The latter are expressed in purchase orders; the former may be significantly different in both timing and quantity. A knowledge of these will be most helpful to a manufacturing plant trying to give its customers truly great service.

Finance

This group has been focusing its attention on the financial data needed to meet the requirements of the tax and other governmental agencies and to present data in standardized form for the owners (the stockholders). Its relation to operations has been more in the nature of a watchdog to insure that capital is well utilized and budgets are reasonably well met. Unfortunately, data needed for making decisions in running the operation have not been available through the financial systems. This must be included in their primary task. They must begin to help the players instead of concentrating on the scorekeeping.

The Master Schedulers' Job

Obviously some staff work is needed to handle the details involved with revising and distributing the MPS, overseeing its application, reviewing actual performance against it and preparing supporting information for management reviews. The question of how this function should be organized and where it reports is concerning many companies.

In many it is now a low-level clerical operation in material control. This invariably happens in those companies whose interest in the MPS developed only after they installed an MRP program and needed a set of numbers to drive it. This is rarely a good working arrangement. People at this level cannot resist the pressures of executives several organizational levels higher and find themselves pushed and pulled periodically in response to the whims of such executives. (One individual suffered a heart attack as a result). This is a poor arrangement to develop a sound concensus among managers. The result is a nervous wish-list. Those companies making really effective use of the MPS have an individual or small group, often called manufacturing or production planning, responsible for:

1. Reviewing the forecast of customer demand and developing needed changes with the sales and marketing groups.
2. Converting forecast data into production plans.
3. Correlating production plans with shipping budgets and inventory and marketing plans.
4. Developing and maintaining the MPS files, transmitting them to all who need them with necessary explanatory materials.
5. Attending meetings reviewing the MPS, anticipating management's questions and attempting to provide relevant data so that answers can be developed on the spot.
6. Making delivery promises to customers.

7. Evaluating the effects of changes to the MPS suggested by top management.

8. Evaluating the effects of changes to the MPS caused by constraints in material or capacity.

9. Revising the MPS when necessary and providing the files needed to run the MRP programs.

10. Bringing conflicts among organizational groups or in meeting customer orders to top management's attention.

Obviously this is a manager's, not a clerical job. To do it well an individual has to have the respect of top level management and must understand how managers think and the kind of information they need in decision-making. While being comfortable with masses of data, the individual will also have to be able to extract significant problems and trends and understand the sources of data which can be used in helping solve such problems and handle such trends. Individuals holding such jobs have been moving steadily up the organizational ladder; many are now at the vice presidential level.

15. The Future

A Changing Environment

The operation of any manufacturing company will have to be significantly different in the future from the way it has been in the past. Many factors are contributing to these dramatic changes. The principal one is international competition which is intensifying as more Pacific Rim countries become active in serving world-wide industrial markets. Among the developing nations, China can be expected to intensify such competition.

The payback from sound planning comes only when plans are executed properly; planning is necessary but not sufficient. The level of managers in the organization involved in developing plans and the type of cooperation achieved in executing the plans measure the maturity of management in effective business planning and control.

In their marketplaces, management is also becoming more aware that customer relations can be improved if suppliers and customers work much more closely together and the number of suppliers is limited. The mutual benefits to be gained through a partnership instead of an "arms-length relationship" are very significant. These include more timely deliveries, better quality, higher turnover of inventories in both parties and significantly lowered overhead costs. When a certified supplier delivers a product of guaranteed quality directly to the point of use in the customer's facilities, many activities and their expenses are eliminated (receiving, incoming inspection, stores and trucking) plus added benefits result from higher quality components and lowered repair and rework costs. Such savings will offset by many times the higher direct labor rates in the more mature industrial countries like the United States.

Several economic factors are also dictating significant changes in operations. Interest rates will remain high and, in fact, may get even higher. The availability of capital in the equity market will never be as it was in the '50's and '60's. Valuable capital will continue to be diverted to acquisitions and mergers with a slice off the top for the bankers and lawyers instead of being available to provide productive resources. Thus management will have to improve the productivity of capital; they have paid relatively little attention to this in the past. Only an inveterate optimist would assume that inflation rates will stay low for any significant number of years in the future. Nor is it likely that the tax structure will become more favorable for industry. All of these factors intensify the need for better management of capital assets.

At the same time, the increasing rate of change in technologies of products and processes will make the future a more rapidly changing environment. The proliferation of types of new raw materials and the development of new manufacturing processes utilizing laser and other technologies will lead to much shorter product life cycles. Future products will also be characterized by a proportionately higher material content. This increases the pressure to improve the productivity of material usage which has also received too little attention in the past.

The important trend of the future is already visible. This is the focus on shortening the manufacturing cycle time. Why should it take months to move through a factory products which are worked on only a few hours? This is almost invariably the norm not the exception. The successful company of the future will move its products rapidly through the plant and will react quickly and flexibly to changing customer requirements. There is enough evidence already to be able to state without qualification that such shortening of cycle times IS POSSIBLE IN ANY INDUSTRY.

There is no doubt that this is far easier to do in some industries than in others. The high-volume, mass production, repetitive type of manufacturing lends itself most easily to shortening manufacturing cycles. Dramatic reductions have been made, however, in other industries. Cycle times have been reduced, for example, from four months to two weeks for large, custom engineered products and from six weeks to two days for electronic equipment.

Such cuts cannot be made by reducing only the direct working time of people on products or machines on components. Improvements in productivity of direct labor and machines will continue to be made but these are now only a very small factor in the total cycle time reduction process. The bulk of wasted time in manufacturing occurs in storerooms and work-in-process. Attacks on such waste result in greatly improved productivity of capital and material.

Just-In-Time

The phrase "Just-In-Time" has been adopted widely to describe those activities focusing on reductions of manufacturing cycle time. Like all buzzwords, however, widespread use of the phrase by managers who do not completely understand its meaning and intent have led to serious misconceptions about its applicability to their types of business. Reference 21 in the Bibliography covers a round-table discussion of Just-In-Time as it is being applied to all types of industries and is a thorough treatment of the topic for those interested in more detail. Referred to variously as a strategy, process or new way of life, Just-In-Time focuses on all waste which slows down the manufacturing process.

The successful implementation of Just-In-Time in a company will be dependent not on solving technical problems but rather on developing the correct management attitudes and understanding. Many pieces of conventional wisdom must be challenged and seen in their true light as fallacies. Among these are: "Inventory is an asset", "There is some right amount of inventory for any business" and "Idle time of people or expensive machines is wasted". In addition to these few, there are many more examples of common beliefs which need to be refuted in order to run a manufacturing plant the way it should be.

This is the most difficult of all education to accomplish. To illustrate the difficulty in overcoming such habits of thought, Figure 19 gives an example of a level schedule for production of three products during a month. This is typical of the schedules developed by the majority of people to whom the situation is explained. The three products have monthly requirements as shown in the second column. The total load can be handled by the facilities which have adequate capacity. A level schedule to most people means an equal amount of work to be done each week. Most people also think of production in batches with minimum time devoted to changing over machines so the schedule of producing all "A's", all "B's" and then the "C's" is the most frequent suggestion.

FIGURE 19
LEVEL SCHEDULE #1

Product	Monthly Requirements	Week 1	Week 2	Week 3	Week 4
A	80	40	40		
B	60			40	20
C	20				20
Load	160	40	40	40	40
Capacity	160	40	40	40	40

A small portion of the people looking at this situation would develop the schedule shown in Figure 20. Obviously, such individuals have less concern for batch sizes and setup times and

FIGURE 20
LEVEL SCHEDULE #2

Product	Monthly Requirements	Week 1	Week 2	Week 3	Week 4
A	80	20	20	20	20
B	60	15	15	15	15
C	20	5	5	5	5
Load	160	40	40	40	40
Capacity	160	40	40	40	40

more concern for having all products available for customers in every week. Very few people, however, not one in a thousand, would suggest that the best and most level schedule would be to run EVERY DAY the sequence A — B — C — A — B — A — B — A. Obviously, to produce such a sequence, a plant would have to have practically no setup times for changing over equipment, an adequate supply of components in the proper mix and the stability of this schedule over some reasonable period like one or two months. This is, of course, typical of the way automobile assembly plants are scheduled. Unfortunately, the plants supplying these assembly plants with major components are still run on a batch basis with the corresponding fluctuations and problems. Obviously also, plants run to such final assembly schedules could have smooth production of components if there were equal flexibility in the processes by which they were made.

Just-In-Time is a strategy for attacks on the elimination of waste in all phases of a company's operations including sales and marketing, engineering and finance as well as manufacturing. Even greater difficulties are encountered among managers in these other functions. To redirect the thinking of such executives, it is vital that the chief executive officer understand not only the possiblities of the total approach but also the feasibility of applying it in his operations. **Every successful Just-In-Time installation is characterized by a chief executive officer who is deeply involved and thoroughly committed to improving his operations by this route.**

Keys To Success

A few elements can now be identified as fundamental requirements for success in the future:

1. Top management commitment. As just discussed in the preceeding paragraphs, this commitment to improving manufacturing operations rather than to selling them off or buying others is essential to a continuation of manufacturing as a strong source of real wealth in the United States or any other industrial country.
2. Education and training. Since so many of our old practices have to be unlearned and so many long-held ideas need to be challenged and refuted, a basic need exists for education throughout all levels of management and the workforce. The game has changed and the players need new skills as well as a new strategy for winning.
3. A dedication to continual improvement. No one-time project, quick-fix gimmick or magic program can accomplish the kinds of change needed to remain strong and keep growing in tomorrow's competitive manufacturing environment. Change for its own sake, however, is simply another form of waste. What is needed is constant pressures in all of the organizational functions to change **in the direction necessary to streamline and coordinate all supporting as well as direct manufacturing activities.**

The Requisite Redirection

Among the most difficult yet most essential changes needed are:

1. Redirection of design engineering toward products which lend themselves to flow line production.
2. The change in industrial engineering toward processes which resemble petroleum refineries.

3. Change from multi-source, competitive suppliers to single-source co-makers with continual sharing of information on the requirements of each, working together for frequent deliveries and achievement of 100% quality.

4. A revision of cost accounting processes from batch costing of material and labor on workorders to process costing, accumulating total material and labor by product by period and allocating overhead costs by cycle time, not labor cost.

5. A maximum of participative decision making. Staff professionals like engineers, tool and die designers and quality assurance statisticians must see their roles as supportive of employee groups focusing on problem solving. Instead of being the experts who initiate all actions in their own realms, these professionals must assist others to understand their particular techniques and skills so that these can be applied by more people to more problems.

6. Constant emphasis on flow. Anything sitting or not being worked on must be suspect. This principle must be applied to paperwork as well as to physical materials in the product lines. Waste of time, whether it be in physical manufacture or communications, must be minimized.

The future will be fertile or futile depending upon managers' abilities to redirect the efforts of their people toward the revolutionary improvements in operations which are possible today. All companies in all countries have the same number of hours in a day. Basic materials, machinery and other physical resources are available to everyone. At the levels required in normal manufacturing, the availability or lack of energy is not a controlling factor. The unique resource available to any company is its people, particularly its management. These will determine whether or not their companies enjoy success or disappear from the scene.

BIBLIOGRAPHY

1. Brenizer, Ned W., "The Bottom Line Begins at the Top", Production and Inventory Management, 1st Quarter, 1977.
2. Buffa, Elwood S., "Meeting the Competitive Challenge", Dow Jones-Irwin, 1984.
3. Corey, E. Raymond, "Procurement Management: Strategy, Organization And Decision-Making", CBI Publishing Company, Inc., 1978.
4. De Meyer, Arnoud, "Defining A Manufacturing Strategy — A Survey of European Manufacturers", First World Congress of Production and Inventory Control, Vienna, Austria, May 1985.
5. Donovan, R. Michael, "Manufacturing Strategy: A Competitive Weapon", Proceedings 1985 APICS International Conference.
6. Drucker, Peter F., "Management: Tasks, Responsibilities, Practices", Harper & Row, 1973.
7. Erst, Richard S., "Closing The Top Management Loop Throuogh Four-Dimensional Planning", Proceedings 1984 APICS International Conference.
8. Everdell, Romeyn, "Master Scheduling: Its New Importance in the Management of Materials", Modern Materials Handling, October 1973.
9. Everdell, Romeyn, "Master Production Scheduling", APICS Training Aid.
10. Geneen, Harold, "Managing", Doubleday & Company, Inc., 1984.
11. Hayes, Robert H. and Wheelwright, Steven C., "Restoring Our Competitive Edge: Competing Through Manufacturing", John Wiley & Sons, 1984.
12. Holstein, William K. and Sprague, Linda G., "Production Planning And Control Systems: Exactly What Is 'Top Management Support'?", First World Congress of Production and Inventory Control, Vienna, Austria, May 1985.
13. IBM Publication, "Master Production Schedule Planning", Volume III, Chapter 4, of COPICS, Publication #G320-1976.
14. Kuilman, M., "Is There A Next Logistics Generation?", First World Congress of Production and Inventory Control, Vienna, Austria, May 1985.
15. Mather, Hal, "Reschedule the Reschedules You Just Rescheduled — Way of Life for MRP?" Production and Inventory Management, 1st Quarter, 1977.
16. "MRP Symposium", Production and Inventory Management, 2nd Quarter, 1977.
17. Plossl, George W. and Wight, Oliver, "Material Requirements Planning by Computer", APICS Special Report, 1971.
18. Plossl, George W., "The Best Investment — Control, Not Machinery", Production and Inventory Management, 2nd Quarter, 1977.
19. Plossl, George W., "Production and Inventory Control: Principles and Techniques", 2nd Edition, Prentice-Hall, Englewood Cliffs, NJ, 1985.
20. Plossl, George W., "Production and Inventory Control: Applications", George Plossl Educational Services, Inc., Atlanta, GA, 1983.
21. Plossl, George W., "J. I. T. — A Special Roundtable", George Plossl Educational Services, Inc., Atlanta, GA, 1985.

22. Skinner, Wickham, "Manufacturing — Missing Link In Corporate Strategy", Harvard Business Review, May-June 1969.
23. Skinner, Wickham, "The Focused Factory", Harvard Business Review, May-June 1974.
24. Thomas, Hayward, "Strategic Planning: Essential to the 'Factory of the Future", Proceedings Synergy '84 Conference.
25. Thurow, Lester C., Editor, "The Management Challenge — Japanese Views", MIT Press, Cambridge, MA 1985.
26. Wheelwright, Steven C., "Japan — Where Operations Really Are Strategic", Harvard Business Review, July-August, 1981.

INDEX

Achieving corporate objectives
design engineering view, 4
manufacturing view, 4
marketing view, 4
research and development view, 4
Action notices
reducing number, 38
Adjustments to the MPS
causes , 28
fences to limit, 59
in MPS zones, 53
nervousness, 75
Affiliate plant requirements
planning in MPS, 30
Affiliate plants
rough-cut capacity requirements planning, 49
Aircraft, 39
All-stars, not team, 78
Allocations
first step in execution process, 60
for determining shortages, 60
warehouse replenishment systems, 44
Answering customer inquiries
forcing a match with MPS, 54
using the MPS, 67
Arsenal of democracy, 1
Aspirin, 41
Assembly schedules
part of execution process, 52
Automobile
assembly plants, 84
tires, 43
Automobiles, 39, 74
Availability of capital, 81

Ball-bearings, 46
Basic principles
of manufacturing operations, 1
Bearings, 37

Bill of labor
for affiliate plants, 49
for capacity planning, 46
for key suppliers, 47
precision unnecessary, 47
Bucketless systems
illusion of precision, 33
Budgeting
direct and indirect labor budgets, 68
expenses , 68
integrating all budgets, 68
realistic versus ideal, 68
using the MPS and MRP, 67
Buses, 39
Business computer
in inventory management, 19
Business planning, 12
actions of competitors, 12
horizon and questions, 5
product families, 12
share of market, 12
steps, 12

Capacity and priority planning
inter-dependency, 71
Capacity limitations
consideration in master scheduling, 19
effects of overloading, 67
Capacity planning
using the MPS, 66
Capacity requirements planning(CRP)
detailed, 50
rough-cut, 45
Chain, 37
Chain saws, 73
Changing production levels, 17
Changing the MPS
alternatives to, 63
Charter of business, 8
in strategic planning, 5
Chemicals, 37, 41, 43, 74
China, 81
Combination of options
handling in MPS, 39

Comparing required and available capacity
insuring realistic MPS, 50
Computer assisted design(CAD)
problems with, 56
Computer assisted engineering(CAE)
failure to integrate, 56
Computer assisted manufacturing(CAM)
failure to integrate, 56
Consensus among managers
using the MPS, 78
Construction machinery, 37
Consumer products, 41
Conventional wisdom as fallacies, 82
Corporate objectives
customer service, 4
profits, 4
rate of growth, 4
return on investment, 4
share of market, 4
Customer delivery promises
forcing a match with MPS, 54
using modular bills of material, 39
using the MPS, 67
Customer orders
used as the MPS, 39
making delivery promises, 39
Customer service
achieving desired levels, 4
satisfying real needs, 55
using safety stock, 18
Customer-company relations
teamwork to improve, 81
Customers marketplace intelligence
ways to gather, 12
Customers needs versus wants, 10

Dampening nervousness in plans
with firm planned orders, 75
Design engineering
adherance to schedule, 8
coordination with marketing, 8
in business and production planning, 6
objectives, 4

primary role, 78
strategies, 9
Developing common game plan
hierarchy of planning, 4
using the MPS, 71
Developing nations, 81
Direct labor costs, 2
Distribution Requirements Planning
for branch warehouses, 43
See also: time-phased order points
Doors, 58
Dummy product
for bills of labor, 47

Education and training
key to success, 84
need for new skills, understanding, 84
need for top management, 2
Excellence in operations
requirements for, 4
just-in-time, 82
Execution process
first step, 60
separating from planning, 54

Farm equipment, 37
Fences in the MPS
cease planning, start execution, 61
for stability of plans, 59
location, 60
Finance
primary role, 79
strategies, 10
Financially-oriented managers
in 1970s, 1
in 1980s, 2
Fine chemicals, 41
Finishing schedules
part of execution process, 52
Firm planned order, 75
avoiding nervousness, 28
Flexibility planning
in resource planning, 67

using cushions in MPS, 55
Formats
bills of labor, 46
MRP display, 66
of the MPS, 34
production plan, 13
rough-cut CRP, 48
time-phased prder point, 27
Front-ended MPS
effects on priorities, 63

Future
changing environment, 81
fertile or futile?, 85
product designs , 81
requirements for success, 82
shorter manufacturing cycle times, 82
requirements for success, 84
teamwork with suppliers , 81

Garments, 37
Gears, 37, 38
Government
antagonistic, 1
cooperative, 1
assistance, 3

Hand tools, 37, 41
Handle on the business
for top management, 78
Hoists, 39
Home appliances, 37
Horizons
business plan, 5
master production schedule, 5, 31
minimum for MPS, 31
production plan, 5
strategic plan, 5

Industrial fans, 58
Inflation, 81
Integrating MPS and production plans, 36
Interest rates, 81

Intermittent demand
spare parts, 29
International competition, 81
Inventories
planning with seasonal production, 16
to level skilled labor demand, 16
Just-in-time, 82
focus on waste, 82
implementation, 82

Keys to success
continual improvement, 84
education and training, 84
top management commitment, 84

Labor unions, 1
power and influence declining, 2
Lead times
effect on MPS horizon, 31
Level schedule
example, 83
importance in operations, 83
various views, 83
Levelling production rates
for skilled labor, 16
value of, 14
Long range plan, 4
Lot-sizing
in the MPS, 26

Machine tools, 39
Maintenance of the MPS, 63
Make-to-order operations
S-P-I report, 13
Make-to-order product planning
using time-phased order points, 27
Make-to-order products
backlog of customer orders, 23
overplanning, 58
Make-to-stock operations
S-P-I report, 13
Make-to-stock product planning
using time-phased order points, 27

potential revisions, 23, 24
process limitations, 30
relation to other plans, 52
relation to production plan, 21
released finished goods orders, 25
replacement parts, 29
revision example, 23
role of, 19
safety stocks, 25
separate files to compare actual orders, 35
simulating changes in, 64
sources of MPS data, 22
too easy to change computer files, 35
unreliable data, 31
using family bills of material, 37
using firm customer orders , 22
using modular bills of material, 32, 39
variable-length time buckets, 34
variations, 37
what it is, 20
what it is not, 21
when not to use customer orders, 23
zones, 33
Master schedulers' job, 79
Master scheduling, 18
coordinating organization functions, 21
make-to-order products, 24
make-to-stock products, 24
objectives, 21
task of top management, 19
Material requirements planning(MRP)
format, 66
input required, 19
using forecasts to drive, 19
Monitoring factory performance
using the MPS, 69
MPS variations
assemblies, 41
branch warehouses, 43
combinations of stocked and make-to-order products, 40
continuous or high volume production, 43
major products built for stock, 37
major units custom-built to order, 39

Make-to-stock products
backlog of customer orders, 23
example of MPS, 23
family groupings for MPS , 37
overplanning, 57
seasonal demand, 37
Management policies, 4
Manufacturing
strategies, 9
Manufacturing cycle times
benefits of shortening, 82
effect on plan validity, 55
Manufacturing planning and control systems
development , 1
Manufacturing plans
cushioning against changes, 55
improving validity, 54
Marketing
primary role, 78
strategies, 9
Master production schedule(MPS), 18
a plan, not a schedule, 20
adjusting for constraints, 29
affiliate plants requirements, 30
capacity demands, 25
capacity limitations, 30
changing inventory totals, 25
comparing actual customer orders, 24
considerations in developing, 22
consuming with booked orders, 24
daily time buckets, 20
definition, 20
drives material planning, 65
effects of neglecting, 19
forecast of spare parts sales, 29
freezing a portion, 59
horizon , 31
in finished goods replenishment system, 23
levelling workload, 26
lot-sizing, 26
manufacturing cycle times, 26
not sales forecast, 28
options stating quantities of product, 26

many products built for stock, 37
many products made to order, 39

Nervousness of the plan, 76

Objectives of production planning, 13
Order point
contrast to material requirements planning, 65
factors in, 18
major failing, 19
no common game plan, 71
using when MPS data unreliable, 31
Organization, 77
Overplanning
example with options, 57
for flexibility, 40, 56
for make-to-order products, 58
power of, 59
versus overstating, 74

Pacific Rim countries, 81
Packaging materials, 41
Paints, 41
Pareto principle
application to master scheduling, 38
Past-due MPS requirements
problems in planning, 63
Pharmaceuticals, 37, 41
Photographic film, 41
Planning hierarchy
business plan, 6
long range plan, 4
master production schedule, 6
production plan, 6
strategic plan, 6
Planning worker hiring, training and transfer, 68
Planning parts in sets, 40
Planning versus execution, 52
separating, 54
time relationships, 53
Primary roles of organization groups
design engineering, 78
finance, 79

management must define, 78
marketing, 79
Problems with the MPS, 73
computer software programs, 76
erratic work center loads, 76
finishing schedules, 73
front-ended, 74
invalid input data, 73
nervousness , 75
overstated , 74
Procurement lead times, 18
Product families
choosing in production planning, 14
in business plan, 6
units of measure in production planning, 15
Product life-cycle
effect on production plans, 13
in business planning, 12
Production plan
choosing product families, 14
data for physical capital budget, 13
effect of product life-cycles, 13
focus, 13
make vs. buy analyses, 13
rules for revising, 17
steps in making, 15
typical format, 13
Production planning, 13
additional considerations, 16
cumulative data in, 16
horizon and questions , 5
not a precise process, 17
objectives, 13
Production/delivery ratio, 62
Productivity
of capital, 81, 82
of direct labor and machines, 82
of material usage, 82
Profit planning
using the formal system data, 68
Push systems
for warehouse replenishment, 44

Quarterly ordering system, 18, 19

Radio transmitters, 41
Radios, 43
Railroads in the United States
view of charter, 8
Real wealth
not service industries, 2
sources, 1
Realistic MPS
See also: Master Production Schedule(MPS)
final test, 51
Realistic plans
insuring by management consensus, 78
Redirection needed
cost accounting, 85
design engineering, 85
industrial engineering, 85
participative decision-making, 85
vendor partnerships, 85
of executive thinking, 84
Reliable delivery promises
via the MPS, 21
by forcing a match with MPS, 54
Requirements Alteration
for evaluating MPS changes, 4
Requirements for effective control
sound business and production planning, 6
keys to future success, 84
Research and development
adherance to schedule, 8
in business and production planning, 6
objectives, 4
Resolving conflicts among managers
using the MPS, 78
Resource planning
capacity requirements, 45, 65
fixed capital assets, 31
risk analysis, 67
using the MPS, 67
workforce requirements, 68
Resource profile
See: bill of labor

Risk analysis
in resource planning, 67
Rough-cut capacity requirements planning
advantages, 45
affiliate plants, 49
before running MRP, 50
evaluating alternative plans, 45
for one period, 47
insuring MPS is realistic, 45
spare parts, 49
summary plan, 48
used for trade-off decisions, 50
Rubber products, 37

S-P-I report, 13
Safety stocks
calculation of, 18
in the MPS, 25
Scheduling engineering
using the MPS, 69
Seasonal production plan
alternatives in making, 16
planning inventory levels, 16
Semi-finished product inventory
for flexibility in deliveries, 41
Service industries
pros and cons, 2
Service parts
See: spare parts
Ships, 39
Shortage lists
from formal system, 52
Sources of real wealth
agriculture, 1
extractive industries, 1
manufacturing industries, 1

Spare parts
bill of labor, 49
demand on capacity, 29
intermittent demand, 29
not used in current production, 29
rough-cut capacity requirements planning, 49

used in current production, 29
Specialty chemicals, 40
Spread sheet format for MPS
getting started, 34
Standard of living, 2
Statistical techniques
in forecasting, 18
in inventory management, 18
Strategic planning
compatible strategies of functions, 8
coordination of functions, 8
frequency, 11
horizon and questions, 5
identifying courses of action, 8
statement of charter of business, 8
Strategies
combined in one factory, 10
compatible , 11
competetive, 11
conflicting, 9, 70
for design engineering, 9
for different product lines, 11
for finance, 10
for manufacturing, 10
for marketing, 9
importance of compatible, 8
just-in-time, 82
Structuring bills of material
for product options, 40

Tax structure, 81
Technological changes, 81
Textiles, 37
Time buckets
in the MPS, 32
Time-offset bill of materials
setting minimum MPS horizon, 31
Time-phased order points
as input to the MPS, 26
logic same as MRP, 27
requirements different from MRP, 27
using for make-to-order products, 29
Toiletries, 41

Top management
    commitment is key to success, 84
    handle on the business, 78
    insuring realistic plans, 78
    measures of maturity, 81
    need for education, 2
    uses of the MPS, 77
    using the MPS for control of business, 78
Towels, sheets, pillow cases, 41
Toys, 37
Truck and off-highway vehicle axles, 40
Truck trailers, 39
Trucks, 39
Types of plans, 4

Unit of measure
    product families in production plans, 15
Unplanned demands on capacity, 50
Uses of the MPS, 65
    budgeting, 67
    by top management, 77
    capacity planning, 65
    coordinating major departments, 70
    customer delivery promises, 67
    input to MRP, 65
    management's role, 77
    monitoring factory performance, 69
    profit planning, 68
    resource planning, 65
    scheduling engineering, 69

Valves
    example of family bill of labor, 46
Variable-length time buckets
    problem in MPS, 34

Warehouse inventory control
    Distribution Requirements Planning, 43
    using allocation system, 4
    using push system, 44
    using time-phased order points, 43
Windows, 40, 58

Work ethics
American workers, 1
Workforce budgets
using capacity planning, 68